WOODCARVING
with Rick Bütz
STEP BY STEP

Woodland Warblers

Woodland Warblers

Rick and Ellen Bütz

STACKPOLE
BOOKS

Copyright © 1996 by Rick and Ellen Bütz

Published by
STACKPOLE BOOKS
5067 Ritter Road
Mechanicsburg, PA 17055

All rights reserved, including the right to reproduce this book or portions thereof in any form or by any means, electronic or mechanical, including photocopying, recording, or by any information storage and retrieval system, without permission in writing from the publisher. All inquiries should be addressed to Stackpole Books, 5067 Ritter Road, Mechanicsburg, PA 17055

Printed in the United States of America

10 9 8 7 6 5 4 3 2 1

First edition

Cover design by Tracy Patterson

We have tried to make this book as accurate and correct as possible. Plans, illustrations, photographs, and text have been carefully researched. However, because of the variability of all local conditions, materials, personal skills, and so on, Stackpole Books and the authors assume no responsibility for injuries suffered or damages or other losses incurred that result from material presented herein. Carefully study all instructions and plans before beginning any project.

Library of Congress Cataloging-in-Publication Data

Bütz, Richard.
    Woodcarving step by step with Rick Bütz. Woodland warblers / Rick and Ellen Bütz. — 1st ed.
      p.   cm.
      ISBN 0-8117-2990-7 (pbk.)
    1. Woodcarving—Patterns. 2. Wood warblers in art. I. Bütz, Ellen, 1950– . II. Title. III. Series: Bütz, Richard. Woodcarving step by step with Rick Bütz.
TT199.7.B889   1996
731'.832—dc20
                                                                                                                      95-51134
                                                                                                                        CIP

*To my parents,
Richard and Hectorine Collins,
who taught me the joys of bird-watching*

—Ellen

Contents

Getting Started
1

Blackburnian Warbler
11

Magnolia Warbler
49

Parula Warbler
81

Painting Warblers
115

Resources
151

Making these birds is a great way to learn woodcarving and painting techniques. This book features some of my favorite warblers. I think you will enjoy them, too.

Getting Started

WARBLERS ARE THE JEWELS OF THE NORTH AMERIcan bird world. They are found across the continent, from Florida to Alaska. And, while they are relatively common, they often go unnoticed by casual observers because of their small size and quick, elusive movements. I had enjoyed observing birds for many years before I discovered warblers. I remember the day vividly.

It was an early Adirondack spring day of persistent drizzle. As I was driving along, I suddenly noticed some small, brightly colored birds flitting around a creek. I stopped the car, grabbed my binoculars, and stepped into the woods to take a look. All around me were quick little movements in the trees and bushes. I finally managed to focus my binoculars on one bird and couldn't believe my eyes. It was a beautiful mottled blue with a bright yellow spotted breast: a magnolia warbler, I learned later.

As I was able to focus on other birds, I saw ones with different patterns of blue, yellow, green, white, copper, and muted shades as well. I felt as though I were surrounded by flying Easter eggs as I stood there on the forest's edge. I especially remember a small black-and-white bird with a vibrant orange face and breast. This I discovered was a blackburnian warbler, and I have made him the first project in our book.

Later on, I learned that warblers spend the winter in Central and South America and fly north to breed. They arrive in my neighborhood during early May, and the males begin to establish their territories by singing. This is the best time to see them because the trees are not yet in full leaf, so there is less cover for the birds to hide in. This is also when their colors are the most brilliant, and they often travel together in flocks of many different warbler species. As spring progresses, they spread out, nest, and raise families. By August they begin gathering together for the return journey to warmer climates. At this time their brilliant colors have changed to subdued shades of pale gray, yellow, and dull green, and many species are virtually impossible to tell apart.

Like much of our wildlife, warblers are threatened by civilization encroaching into their habitat. This is especially true in the tropical forests where they spend the winter. Clearcutting and unwise forest management have reduced their wintering grounds to such an extent that ornithologists have noticed a decline in the number of warblers returning north each spring. Development and fragmentation of habitat in their northern nesting grounds have also contributed to the decline in warbler populations.

Warblers are insect eaters; they eat primarily

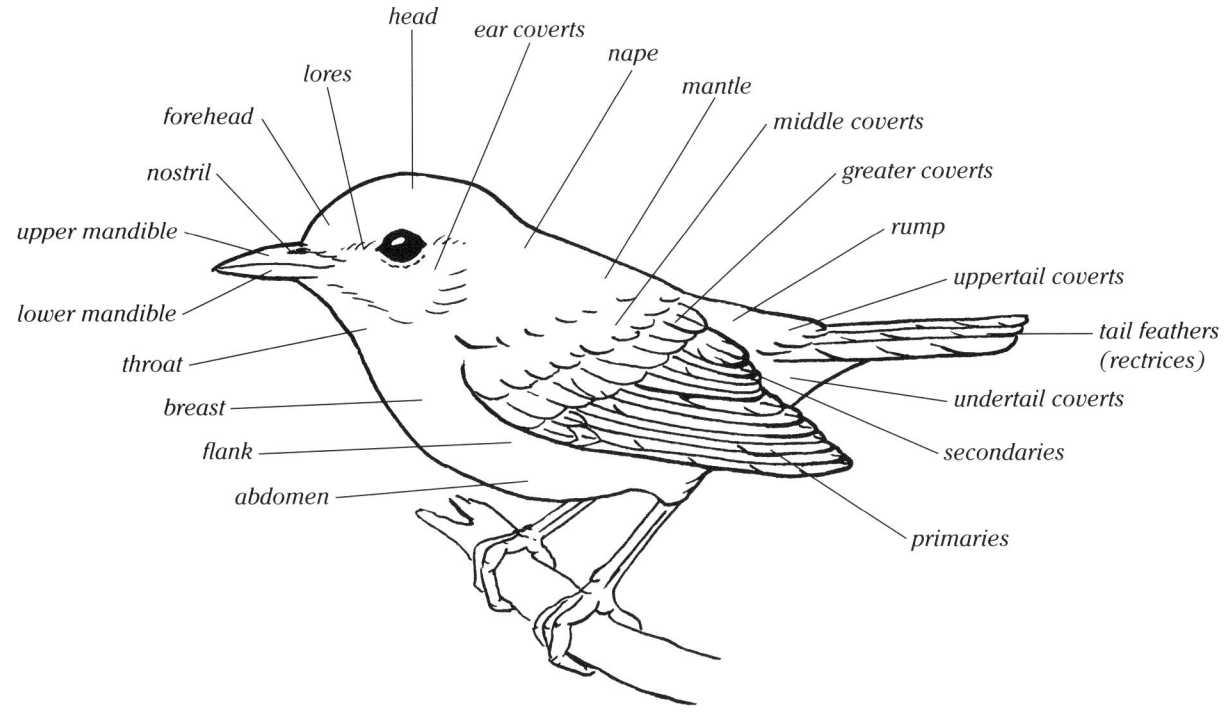

Feather groups on warblers

mosquitoes and other annoying bugs. They often catch them on the wing, a technique known as hawking. They fly from their perch, snatch an insect out of the air, and return to their perch.

The best way to see warblers is to obtain a good pair of binoculars—at least 7-power magnification—and a bird field guide. I recommend *Birds of North America,* published by the Golden Press.

Warblers can be found in virtually any North American habitat, including seasides, lakeshores, swamps, city parks, backyards, farms, deciduous forests, coniferous forests, riverbanks, canyons, and mountaintops. Your local Audubon chapter can advise you and may even arrange day trips for birding. Remember, the more you observe birds in the wild, the more lifelike your woodcarvings will become. So try to spend as much time outdoors as you can observing the birds you want to carve. This is one of the most enjoyable rewards of carving wildlife.

Carving warblers has one major advantage over

other bird subjects. There are literally dozens of warbler species that are nearly identical in shape and size; only the color pattern varies. Therefore, you can use the same carving patterns and methods to create a wide range of birds. Each project in this book captures a shape and pose characteristic of most woodland warblers. Just vary the color scheme. I have included color examples of other common warblers you can adapt to your carving on page 148 of the chapter on painting.

The challenge in wildlife carving is not just to recreate the shape of a species accurately, but also to capture the subtle, elusive qualities that make each bird unique. In this book I will show you how to begin to develop a feeling for this in your own carvings.

Photographs can be helpful for studying certain details, such as the shape of a beak or an eyelid. Don't rely on photographs for planning the entire carving, however, as they can sometimes be misleading. Different lenses can distort shapes, and the camera's split-second shutter speed can "freeze" a bird in an uncharacteristic or awkward pose. For similar reasons I never use dead or stuffed birds as references. Their lack of vitality influences the carving to such an extent that your finished project often looks dead too.

By carving the projects in this book you will learn some of the techniques of realistic songbird carving, including creating feather texture with a woodburning pen and paintbrush, shaping natural-looking eyelids with epoxy putty, and applying paint in a way that brings carvings to life.

The projects in this book are arranged from

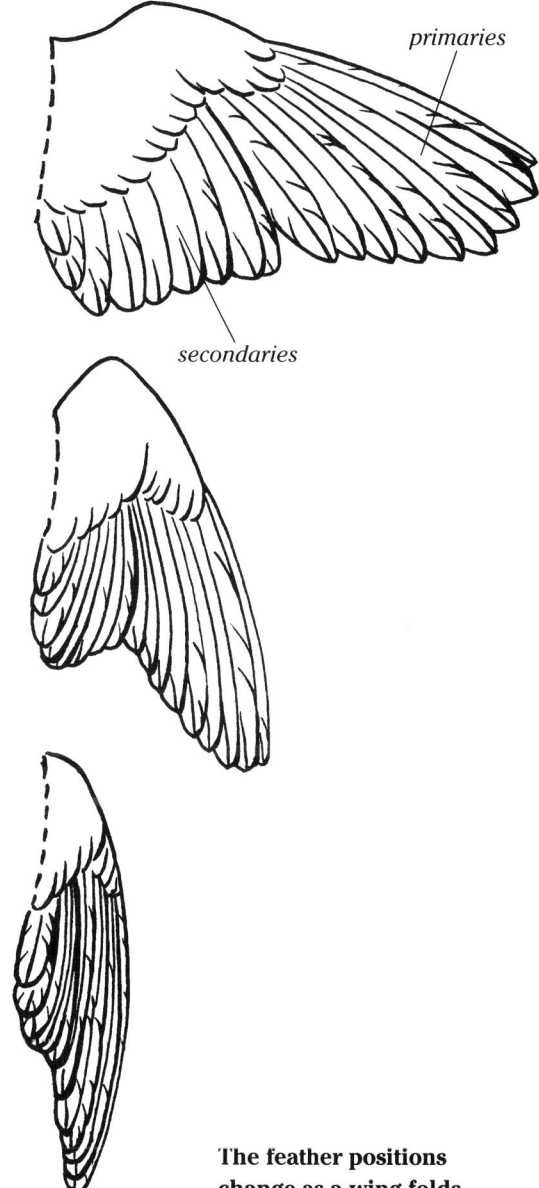

The feather positions change as a wing folds.

simple to more complex. So, if you choose to work your way through the book from beginning to end, you will receive a complete course of instruction in songbird carving techniques.

If you prefer, however, jump right in and start with whichever project appeals to you the most. Each project is designed to stand on its own, with all the information you need to complete it. You will also find full-size patterns and complete painting instructions with each project.

If you have questions about a particular step of the carving, just refer to the section of the book where that technique was first introduced for some additional hints.

WOOD

Around the world, woodcarvers use hundreds of different varieties of wood. In my classes I encourage students to try carving any piece of wood they can get their hands on. Many little-known or local woods can produce excellent carvings.

For carvings like these songbirds, however, I prefer basswood. It has a fine, even grain and smooth texture that hold detail well.

Finding wood can be a problem for beginning carvers. I haunt the local sawmills and buy a year's worth at a time when I find some I like. For most of my projects, I try to get boards about 2 or 3 inches thick.

Often the wood is green, so I dry it myself for a few months before I begin carving. To dry green wood I store it in the loft of my garage or under my workbench. I always put small strips of wood underneath the boards, to lift them off the floor, and between the individual boards in a stack. This allows for good air circulation and ensures even drying.

You may want to start with smaller quantities, however. Your best source of supply will usually be other carvers. Try joining a local carving club. In every group of carvers there is someone who knows someone who has a great supply of wood and will usually be happy to sell you a few pieces.

In addition, most of the mail order companies that sell carving tools also sell small blocks of carving wood. See the Resources section for a list of suppliers.

LIGHTING

You don't need a lot of space or equipment to enjoy woodcarving. All you need to start is a comfortable place to sit and a sturdy table. Natural light is best to carve by, but incandescent light will work well too. Avoid fluorescent light; it is too soft, or diffuse, and does not cast enough shadows to clearly show shapes when you are carving.

TOOLS

The most basic and versatile carving tool is a good knife. I prefer one with a comfortable handle and a short, straight blade. The blade should be about $1\frac{1}{2}$ inches long, made of good carbon steel. You will also find that a few carving gouges are helpful, especially for carving the flying parula warbler's wings.

Throughout this book I will list the gouges that I used for each project. But remember, these are only suggestions. You don't need to purchase every tool I mention. Use what you already have on hand, and feel free to substitute one tool for another of similar size and shape. With a little experimentation you will discover the tools that work best for you, and you can begin developing your own personalized tool kit.

Of course, whatever tools you choose have to be razor sharp. Sharp tools are a joy to work with; they slice off precise chips and leave a smooth, polished surface. Dull tools will crush and tear the wood and make your carvings look crude and splintery no matter how carefully you make the cuts.

Sharp tools are so important that I have devoted an entire book in this series just to sharpening. Refer to it for tips on how to maintain a perfect cutting edge on your tools.

Old woodcarvers know that a sharp tool is safer than a dull one; it requires less force to move it through the wood, and it is less apt to slip and cause injuries.

Sharp tools must be treated with respect, however. Before you begin, take a few minutes to study the following carving methods. Practice on a piece of scrap wood until the techniques begin to feel natural and you have an understanding of how to use your tools safely. This will save you a lot of frustration in the long run.

CARVING
There are two safe ways to carve with a knife. The first is called the paring cut because the basic motion is like peeling a potato. Brace your thumb on the carving and slowly close your hand as you draw the knife through the wood. Keep your thumb positioned on the carving so the knife will not touch it as it cuts through the wood.

The second cut, called the levering cut, is handy for reaching places that are hard to carve with the paring cut. Brace the thumb of your left hand against the back of the knife blade and pivot the knife, using your left thumb as a fulcrum.

These two methods are the best for removing wood safely. They also give you excellent control over the knife so you can shape your carving exactly the way you want to. If you are left-handed, just reverse the hand positions.

For safety, relax and take your time. Don't try to remove big chunks of wood with a single cut. There is an old woodcarver's saying that's worth

The paring cut

Getting Started • 5

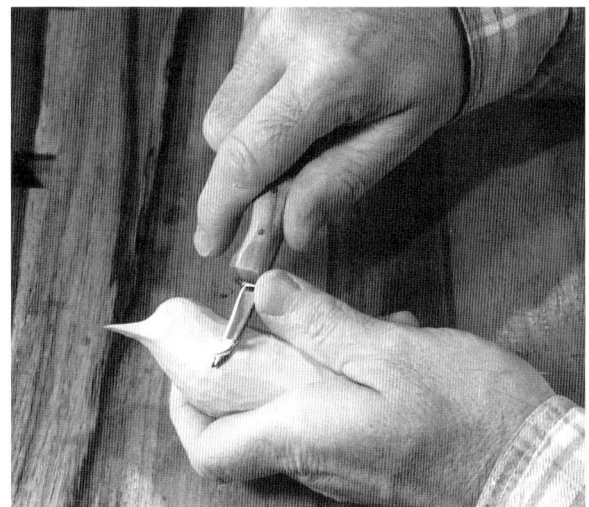

The levering cut

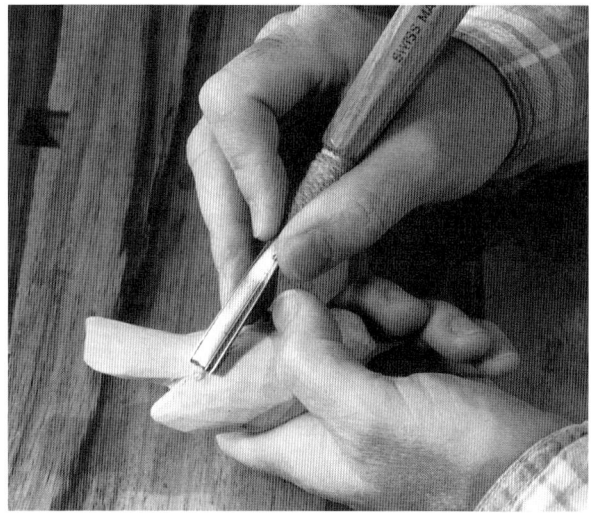

The pencil grip

remembering: "Three small chips are better than one big one."

Above all, never hold the wood in one hand and pull the knife toward you with the full force of your arm. This is very dangerous because you have no control over the knife. Remember, woodcarving is a process of removing small chips of wood with control and precision. When carving, always keep the fingers of both hands braced on the wood for the greatest control and safety.

You can also use woodcarving gouges on these projects, especially for shaping fine details. To do this, the same safety rules apply. Keep the fingers of the hand holding the tool braced on the wood. And never push the tool through the wood with the full force of your arm while holding the carving with your other hand. If the tool slips out of the wood with that much uncontrolled force behind it, the results can be disastrous.

The first technique for using a gouge safely is called the pencil grip. Hold the blade of the tool just like a pencil between your thumb and index finger. These two fingers gently push the blade through the wood in a series of short cuts, while the rest of your fingers are braced against the wood. For even more control, you can rest the shaft of the blade against your middle finger. Notice that the fingers of the hand holding the carving are out of the path of the tool for added safety.

Some types of carvings are easier to shape with gouges if you fasten the wood down to a workbench or sturdy table and hold the tool in both hands. The flying parula warbler's wings are an example of this. For obvious reasons, you should never hold a carving on a bench with one hand while you push a gouge through the wood with your other hand. The carving must be secured to the bench, leaving your hands free to hold the tool.

There are many different ways to fasten a carving to a bench. My own bench has a series of square holes in the top and in the vises. Specially shaped pegs called bench dogs can be placed in these holes to grip the carving while I work.

There are just a few simple rules for safe gouge use. First, fasten the carving down before you begin work. Second, keep both hands on the gouge. One hand usually guides the tool while the other provides the power to move it through the wood.

Finally, with gouges, always carve away from yourself. If you need to make a cut from the opposite direction, turn the carving around in the vise. *Never* pull the tool toward yourself.

Once again, take your time, and remove the wood in a series of small cuts rather than one big one. You'll work more safely and have better control of the carving process.

Another useful tool for songbird carving is the woodburning pen. With a woodburning pen you can create realistic feather details by lightly scorching very fine lines into the wood. Although it is possible to carve these lines by making shallow cuts with a 3mm no. 12 V-gouge, the wood-

Keep both hands on the gouge when carving at the bench.

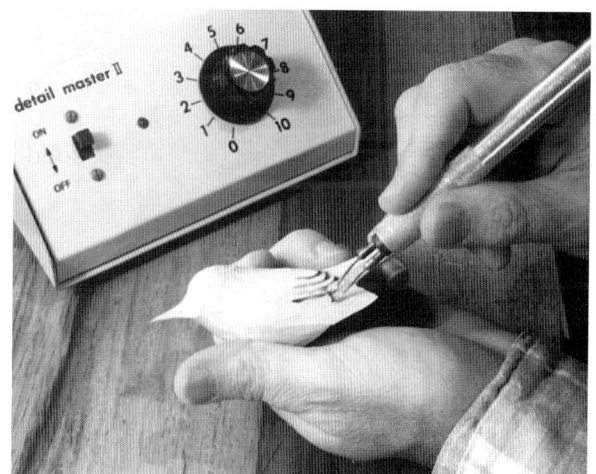

Texturing with a woodburning pen

A magnifier is handy when carving or painting fine details.

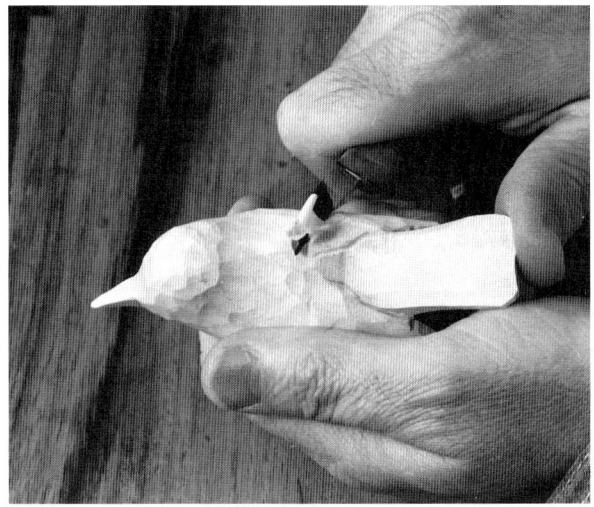

Carving with the grain creates smooth cuts.

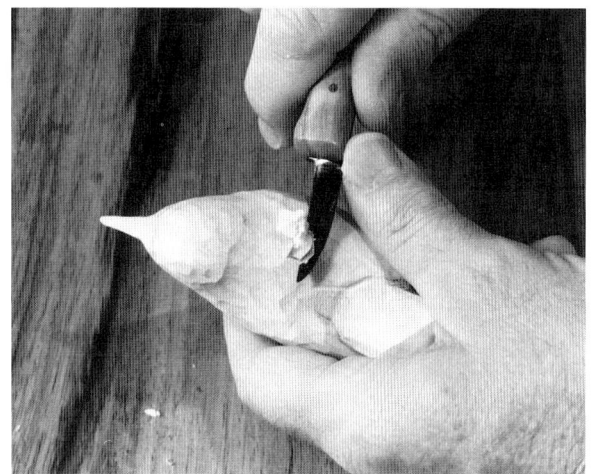

Carving against the grain causes splintering.

burning pen creates a finer, more natural effect. I prefer a pen with an adjustable heat control and interchangeable tips in different shapes for the greatest versatility.

A magnifier is very helpful when you are burning-in fine details with a woodburning pen. I use a 3-power visor that fits comfortably over my regular glasses.

In a sense, woodcarving is different from any other art form because, as a woodcarver, you must learn to work in cooperation with your material. Woodcarving really develops a sense of how to "go with the flow."

Wood is made up of bundles of microscopic hollow fibers called the grain. These tubelike fibers carry nutrients and moisture up and down the trunk of a tree. They also determine the direction you can carve when you are working with a piece of wood.

If you are carving and notice your tool is raising splinters and making a rough crunching sound, even if it is sharp, then you are carving against the grain. Avoid doing this as much as possible.

Instead of carving against the grain, simply carve from the opposite direction. When you carve with the grain, your tool will produce nice, clean shavings and leave a polished surface on the wood.

Carving with the grain is mostly a matter of developing a feel for it. It's a bit like petting a dog or a cat. One way feels right, and the other way doesn't. And like your dog or cat, the wood will quickly let you know which way is right.

Blackburnian Warbler

One of my favorite signs that spring has arrived is the return of the blackburnian warbler *(Dendroica fusca)* who sings in the top of the ancient spruce tree outside my workshop window. The tree is old and ragged, and a forester would take it down in a minute, but the birds love it, so it stays.

Blackburnian warblers' habitat is about 70 feet up in the forest canopy. Because they are so tiny they can be difficult to see despite their brilliant colors.

The blackburnian warbler has been one of my favorite birds ever since I saw my first one. It was early May, and I was watching a mixed flock of migrating warblers catch insects along a little river. Several species of warblers move north together in the spring, and it can be a dazzling sight. I had identified about ten kinds of warblers when suddenly a blackburnian landed on a branch a few feet above my head. I had never seen a bird so strikingly beautiful.

When I looked it up in the field guide, I discovered it was called a blackburnian warbler, or "torch bird." This is an appropriate name, as there is such a vivid contrast between its flaming orange and black markings. Later I found out this warbler was named in 1776 for Lord Blackburn, an English nobleman who never even saw the bird. So, the fact that the name fits is just a lucky accident. At least it wasn't named for the Earl of Sandwich.

This warbler is sitting in a fairly simple position characteristic of all warblers. As you carve it, you will learn the basic techniques for realistic songbird carving. You will also discover how to paint a bird that has vivid contrasts in its coloring. And, you will learn some methods of adding finishing details to the paint that bring the carving to life.

BLACKBURNIAN WARBLER

Tools

Carving knife
8mm no. 5 bent gouge
3mm no. 12 V-gouge
4mm no. 9 gouge
Woodburning pen with a 4-C tip
Drill and bits
Paintbrushes

Materials

Basswood or air-dried white pine
    5 inches by 2 inches by 1¾ inches
4-inch walnut base
1 pair 5mm clear glass eyes
1 pair small cast pewter legs
Spray lacquer
Epoxy putty
Quick-set epoxy
280-grit sandpaper
Gesso
Alkyd paints
    titanium white
    cadmium red medium
    cadmium yellow medium
    ivory black
    burnt umber
Acrylic paints
    titanium white
    ultramarine blue
    ivory black

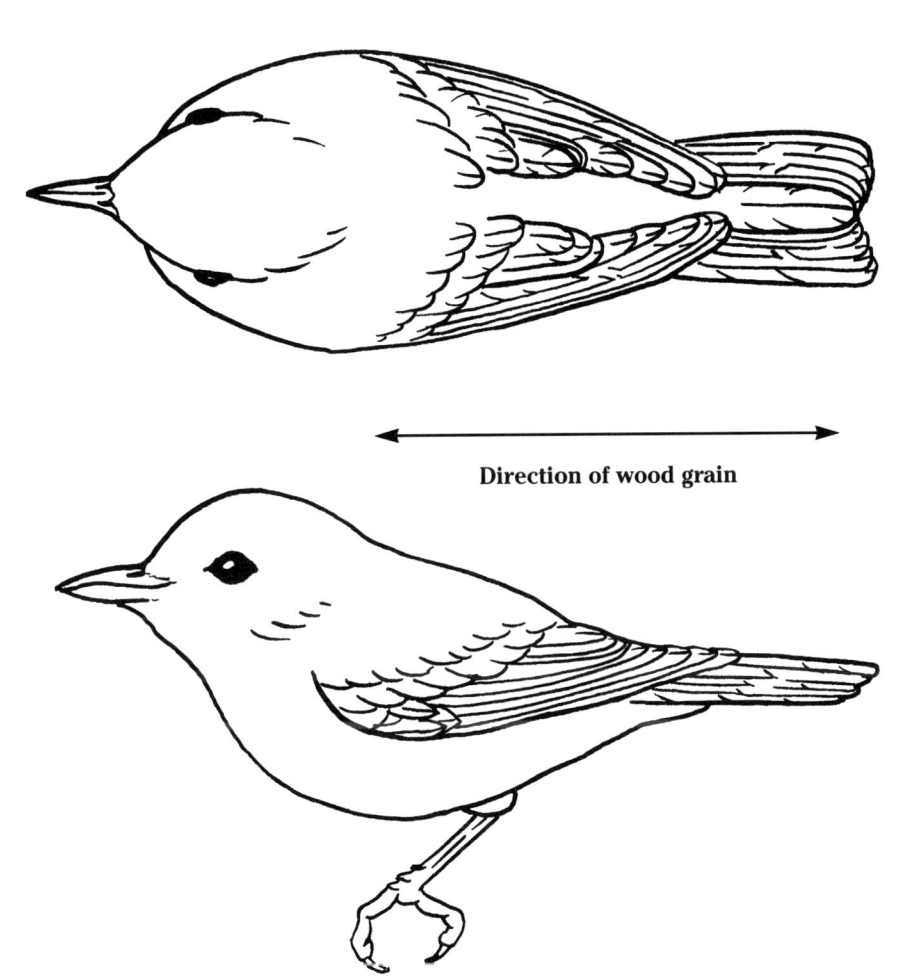

Direction of wood grain

For small birds like warblers I have a slight preference for basswood, although air-dried white pine is also a good choice. Begin with a piece 5 inches long by 2 inches wide by 1¾ inches thick. Be sure the grain runs lengthwise for strength. Trace the profile of the blackburnian warbler on the block with pencil.

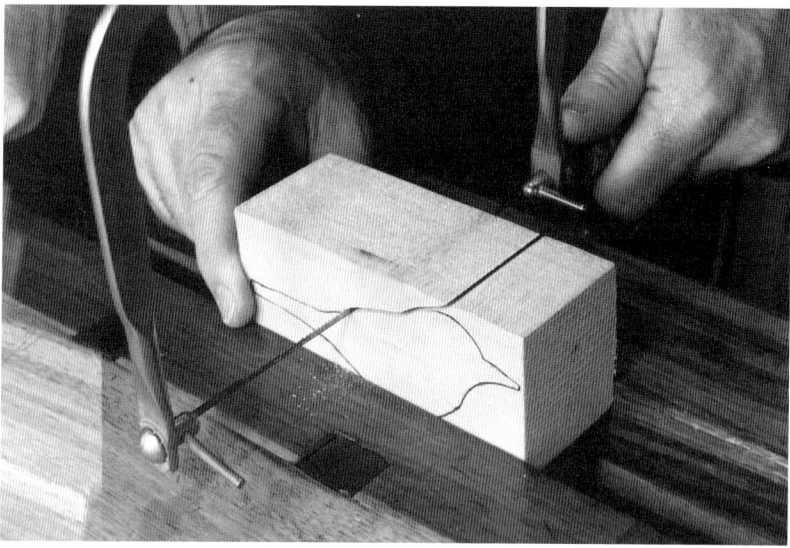

Next, use a band saw or coping saw to cut it out along the outline.

Notice how the grain in the blank runs in the direction of the beak and tail.

I cut out only the profile with a saw. Warblers are so small that it is safer, more efficient, and more fun to remove the rest of the wood by hand.

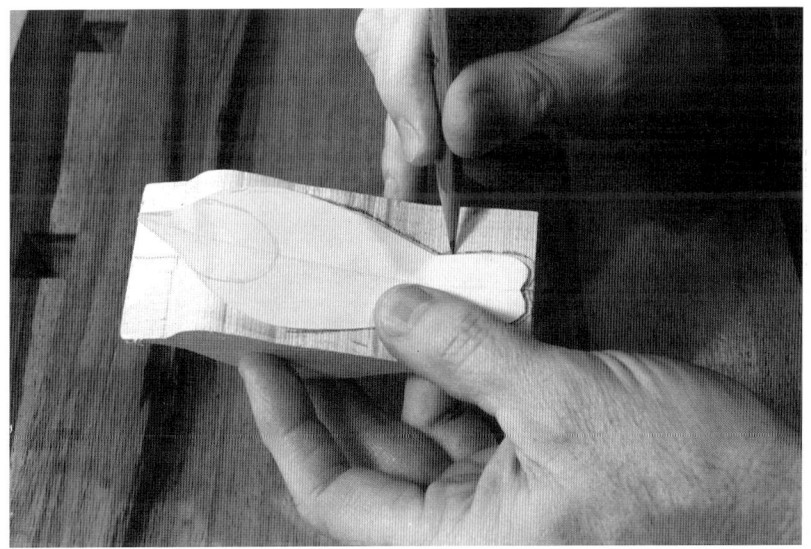

Before you begin carving, draw a centerline on the blank. Then trace the back half of the top pattern onto the top of the blank.

Then, move the pattern forward so that the beak on the pattern coincides with the beak on the blank, and trace the front half of the pattern. You have to do it this way because the top-view pattern in the book is flat, but the back of the blank is curved.

Next, begin removing the excess wood with the carving knife. I prefer a knife with a short, straight blade about 1½ inches long.

Carve away the excess wood outside the guidelines you have drawn. Because the tail is fanned slightly, you have to make one cut down the body to the base of the tail and then carve from the opposite direction to remove a clean chip.

If you carve from the notch between the tail and the body toward the end of the tail, your knife will be cutting against the grain. This may cause some of the wood at the tip of the tail to split off.

If this should happen, don't worry; there is plenty of extra wood on the tail. Simply reshape the tail to a less fanned out position.

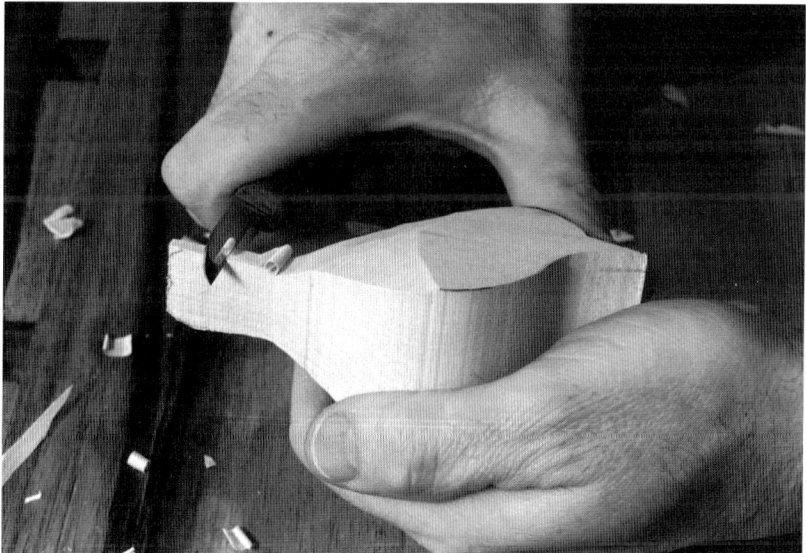

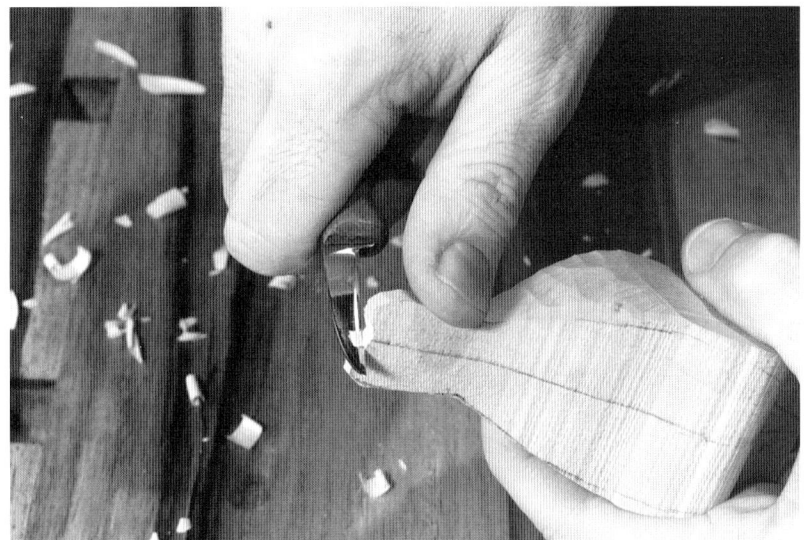

Next, carve the small notch at the tip of the tail. Don't make this cut too deep, as a warbler's tail is not deeply forked.

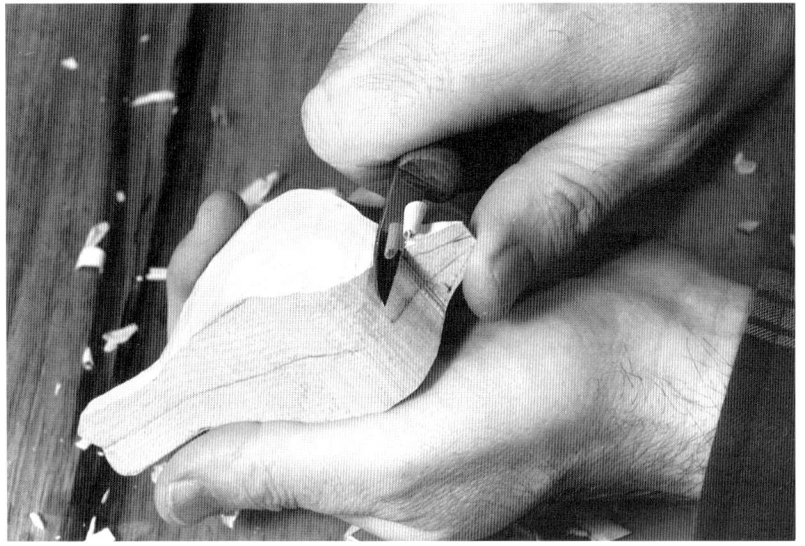

Then, remove the excess wood around the shoulders and head. Don't put too fine a point on the beak; it will be detailed later.

Now that the wood outside the guidelines has been removed, you can begin rounding the carving.

Start by rounding off the corners on the back.

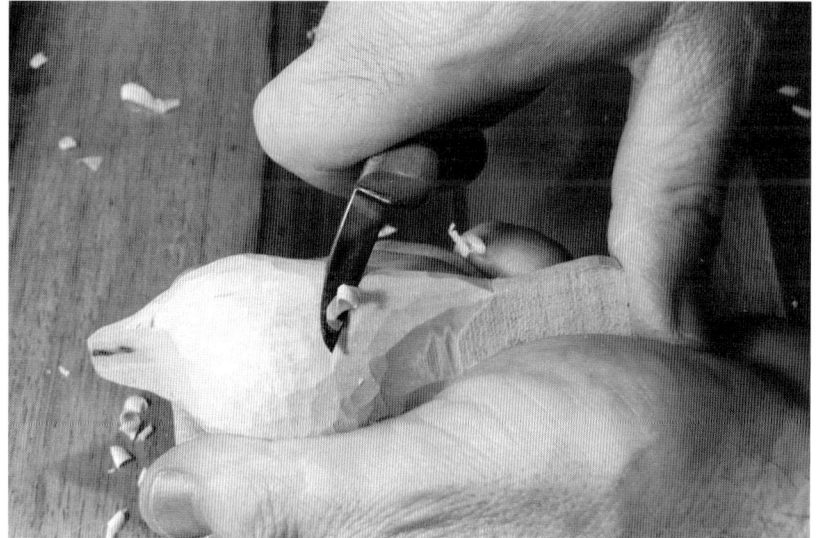

Next, turn the carving over and round the stomach area.

After the body is rounded, pare away the excess wood from the shoulders to the head, narrowing the neck and head. A small songbird's neck is covered by the nape feathers. There is no sharp indentation between the head and the body the way there is in humans, most mammals, or even ducks. Instead, the shapes flow smoothly from shoulder to head.

Round the corners on the top of the head.

Then, round the back of the head.

Next, taper the beak, making it about ¼ inch wide at the base.

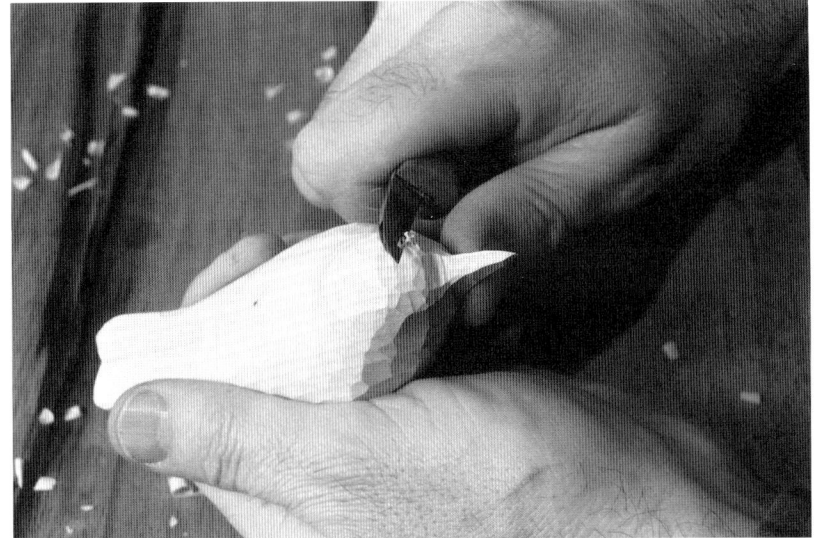

Round the forehead by removing the wood in small, thin chips. The feather texture is very smooth in this area.

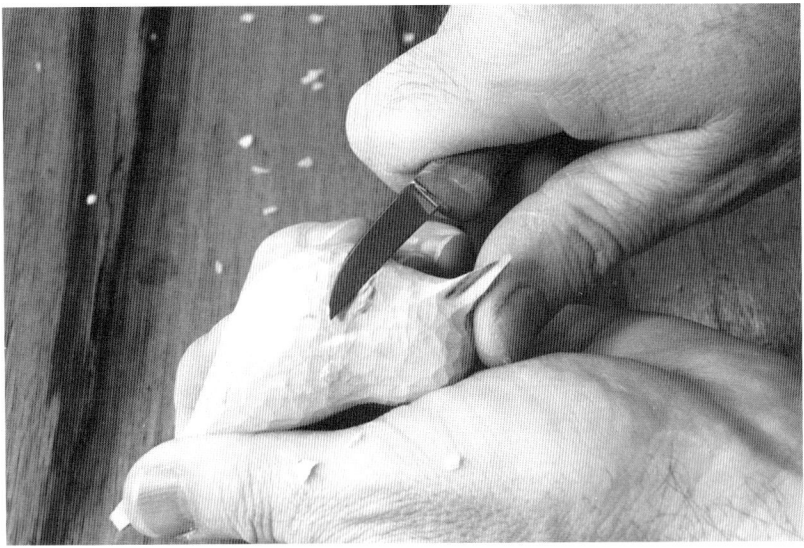

Round off the sharp angles of the throat next, blending the shapes so that they flow smoothly from the chest to the base of the beak.

A warbler's beak is narrow and pointed. It is well suited to the bird's diet of small insects, which it picks from the bark and leaves of trees or catches in midair, a technique called hawking.

Before you begin carving the beak, study the patterns and photos to get a feeling for the shapes. The best way I have found to carve the beak accurately is to shape the side view first. Just concentrate on getting this shape correct before moving on to different views. The beak is approximately $17/32$ inch long (just a little over $1/2$ inch) measured from the forehead to the tip.

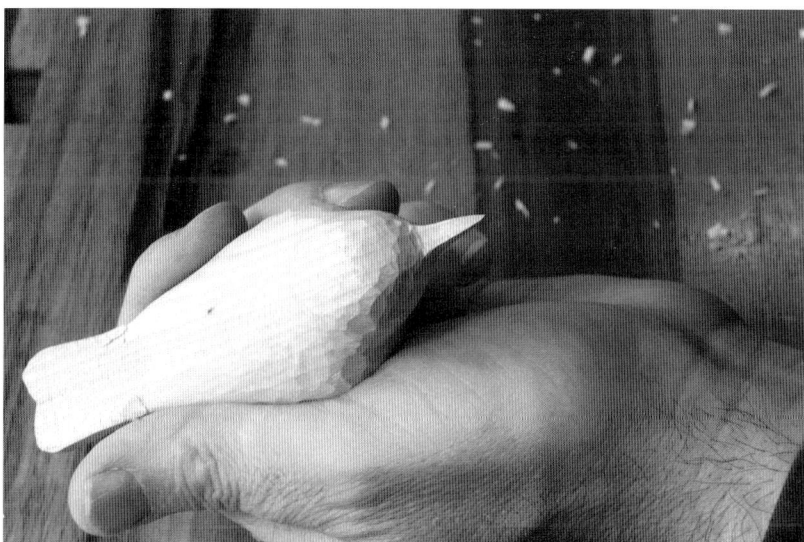

Next, look at the beak from the top and adjust the shape to make it slender and tapering. It should be $7/32$ inch wide at the base—about $1/4$ inch.

Blackburnian Warbler • 23

At this point the beak is square in cross section.

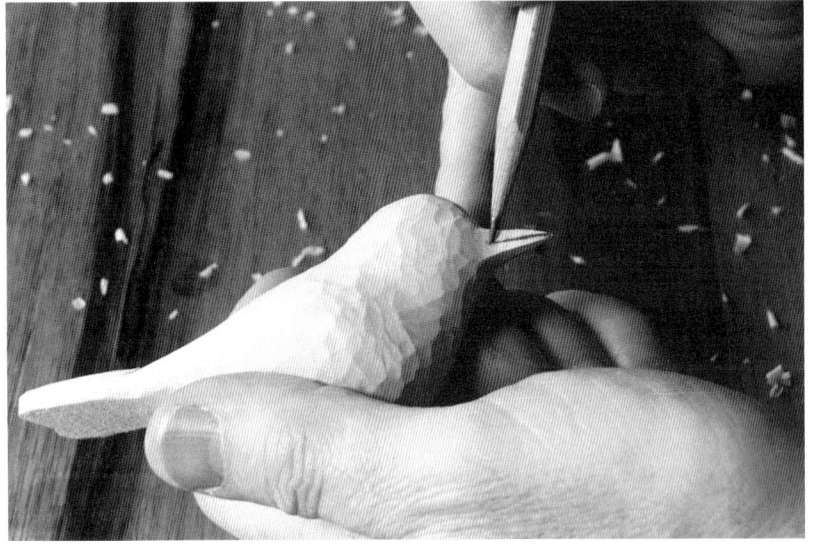

Viewing the bird from the top, draw a guideline down the center of the beak. Then draw a line on each side of the beak indicating the separation between the upper and lower mandibles.

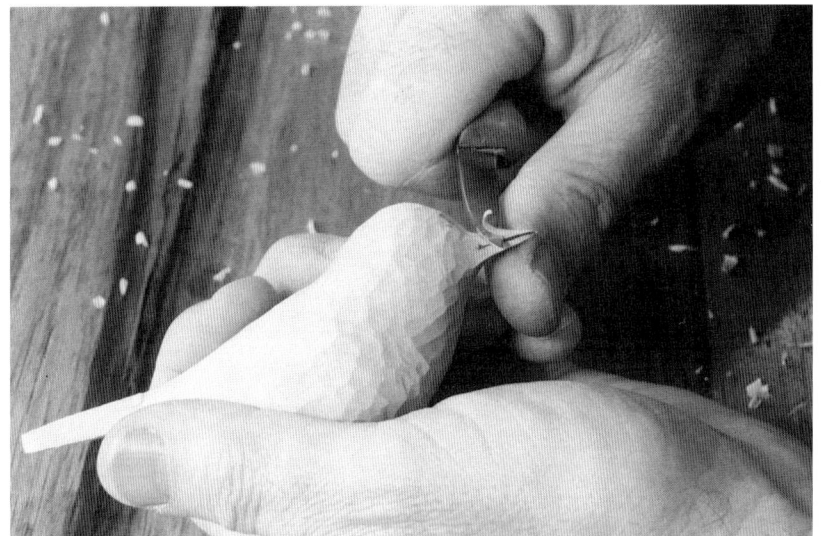

Very carefully pare away the square angle of wood between the top centerline and the sidelines on both the right and left sides. This forms a triangular upper beak.

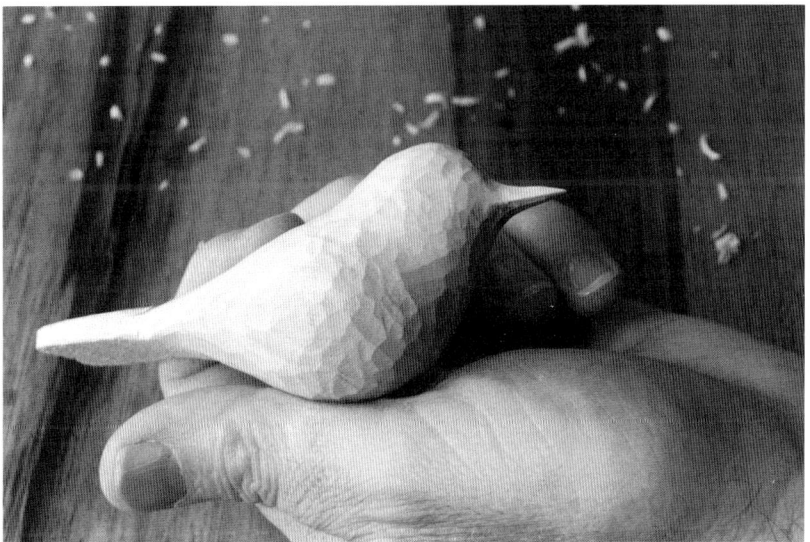

Finally, round the bottom half of the beak. This is the shape of the finished beak.

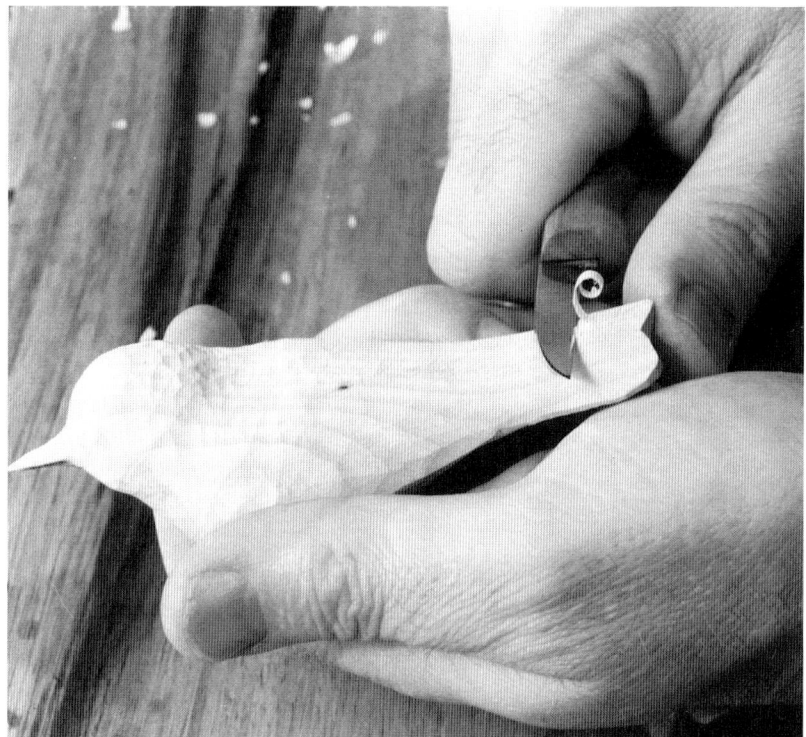

After the beak is done, you can move on to shaping the tail. When you are carving the tail, make sure you are carving with the grain. Each piece of wood is a little bit different, so experiment to find what works best on your particular piece. If you feel your knife starting to dig or it raises splinters, try making the cut from the opposite direction. If you have any questions about this, refer to the part of Getting Started that deals with carving with the grain.

Begin by rounding the top of the tail slightly, cleaning off the saw marks and rounding the sharp angles.

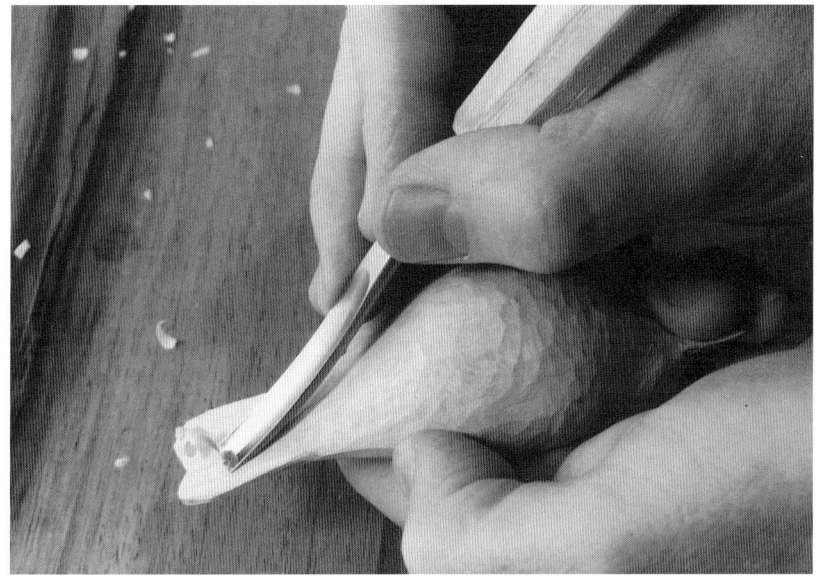

Use a gouge such as an 8mm no. 5 to slightly hollow the underside of the tail. A bent gouge reaches this area more easily than a straight one. Hold the gouge in the pencil grip, making sure the fingers of your other hand are out of the way. If you have not used gouges on small, handheld carvings before, check Getting Started for safety tips before you begin.

Don't make the tail any thinner than 1/8 inch in the center at this point; more wood will be removed later when you carve the wing tips.

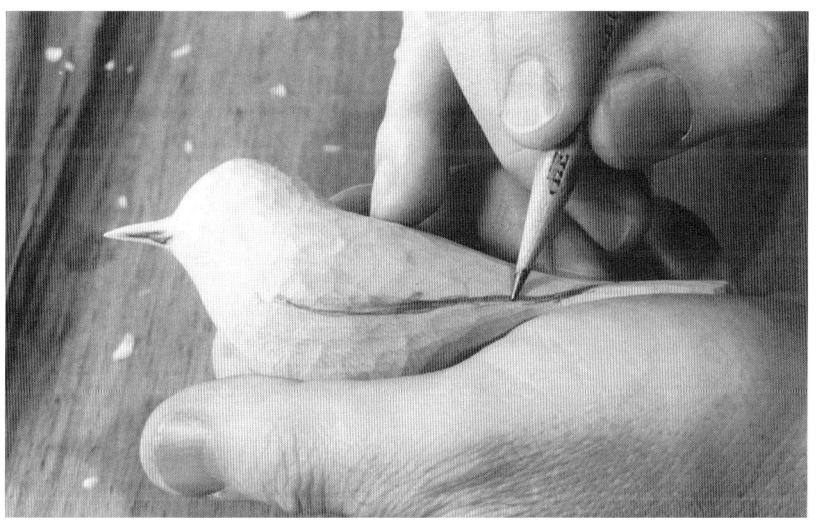

With a pencil, sketch in lines showing the bottom edges of the wings, using the pattern as a guide.

Incise a shallow cut about 1/32 inch deep along the lines with a small V-gouge, such as a 3mm no. 12.

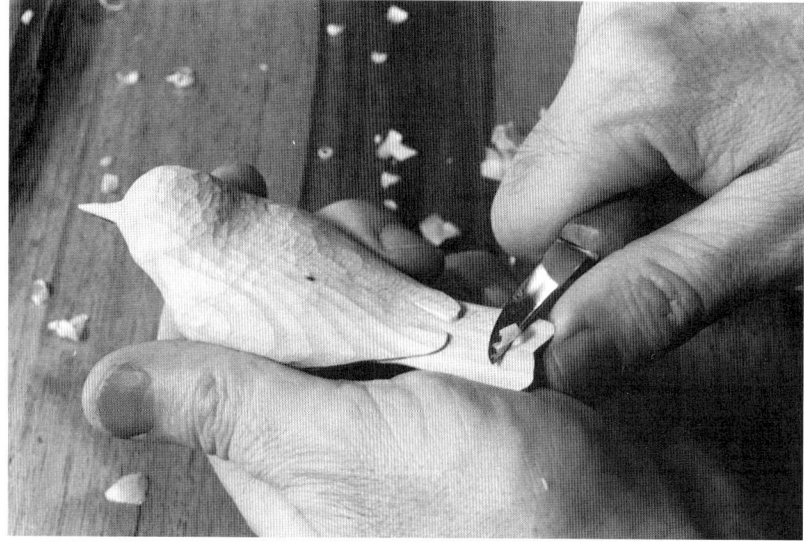

With the carving knife pare away the wood below the cut, leaving the wings raised above the body and tail.

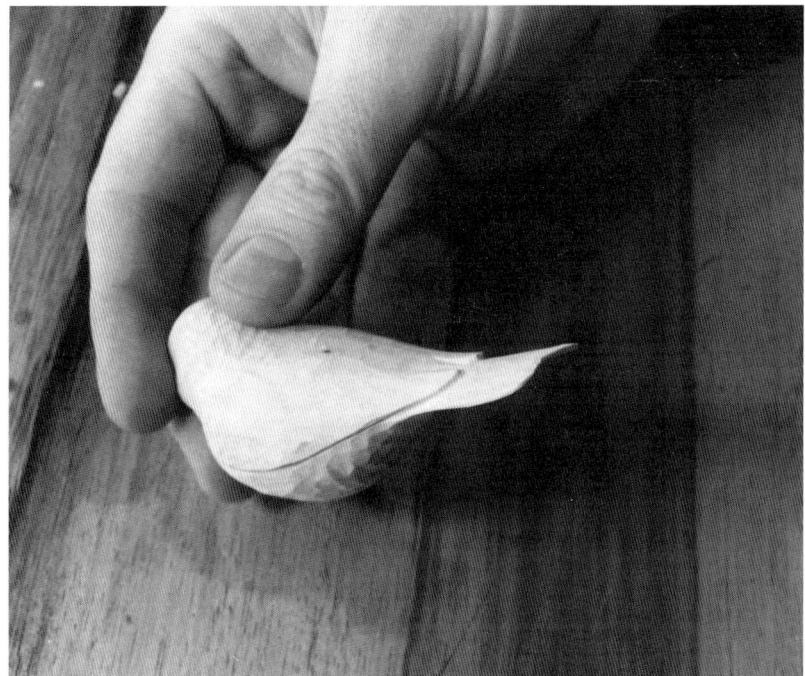

Now, use the carving knife to thin the edges of the tail, including the forked tip. Take your time and be aware of the direction of the grain as you work to avoid splitting the tail. Leave the center of the tail thicker for strength; the thin edges will create the illusion of lightness and delicacy.

The carving work is completed at this point, but before you move on, see that your tool marks are fine and smooth. It's especially important that the knife marks around the head, chest, and back have a fine, regular appearance. After the carving is painted, these tool marks will suggest feather texture.

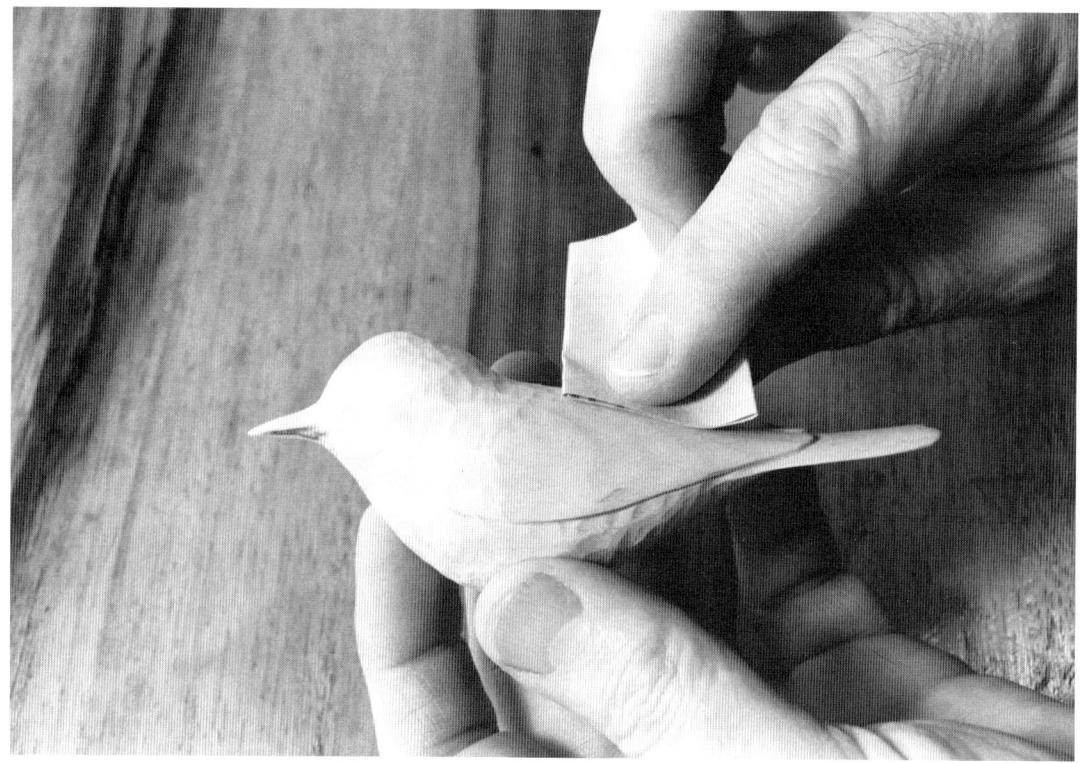

Once you have finished any touch-up cuts with the carving knife or gouges, you can sand the carving lightly. Never sand the wood and then do more carving with a knife or gouge. Fine particles of grit from the sandpaper embedded in the wood fibers will dull your tools very quickly.

I use fine sandpaper, such as 280-grit aluminum oxide or garnet paper, to lightly sand the areas where the flight feathers on the wings and tail feathers will be burned-in later. I recommend sanding these areas to make the feather edges appear more even when they are burned-in.

After you have smoothed the wings and tail, carefully smooth the beak. Don't round the angles on the top of the beak or the sides where the upper and lower portions of the beak meet.

Also very lightly sand the rest of the body, softening the edges of the tool marks slightly without smoothing them out. Subtle variations in the surface texture will reflect light more naturally on the finished carving than will a perfectly smooth surface.

Sketch in lines showing the position of the feathers on the wings and tail. Notice that the feathers overlap the way shingles do on a roof. You can see the whole top feather, but only the lower part of the rest.

A warbler has nine primary feathers and six secondary feathers on each wing. There are twelve feathers on the tail. Don't worry about trying to draw them all. On a living bird the feathers overlap irregularly. The amount of separation between individual feathers varies greatly, and some feathers are completely hidden under others.

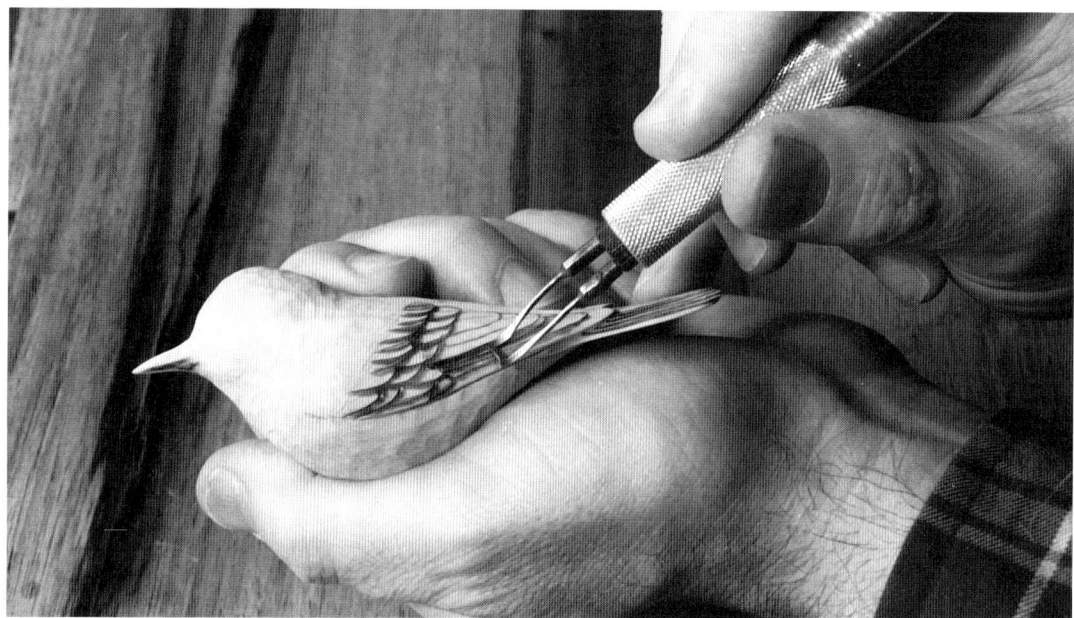

The next step is to use a woodburning pen to detail the feathers of the wings and tail. You could use a small 3mm V-gouge for this, but a woodburning pen gives finer, more natural results.

I prefer a woodburning pen with an adjustable heat control and interchangeable tips, such as the Detail Master II. The adjustable heat control is important because different pieces of wood, and even different parts of the grain on the same piece, require different temperatures to achieve the same effect. I strongly recommend practicing on a scrap of the same type of wood as your carving before you start.

Experiment until you have a temperature setting that will burn a fine, medium to dark brown impression in the wood. Too cool a setting will leave a line in the wood so shallow that it may be obscured by the paint later. Too hot a temperature will actually char the wood and leave coarse, deep lines. A dial setting between 5 and 8 works on most soft woods.

I find a magnifier very helpful when I am burning-in the feather details. The one I use is a 3-power visor that fits comfortably over my regular glasses.

Begin by burning-in the wing coverts and the larger flight feather on the wings. Just hold the woodburning pen the way you would a pencil and draw in the lines.

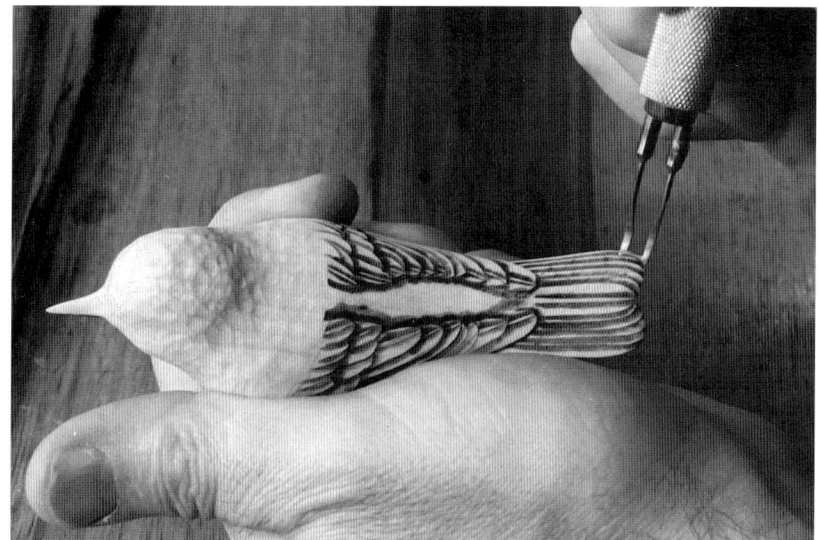

Then do the top of the tail, burning in a central shaft on the top feather.

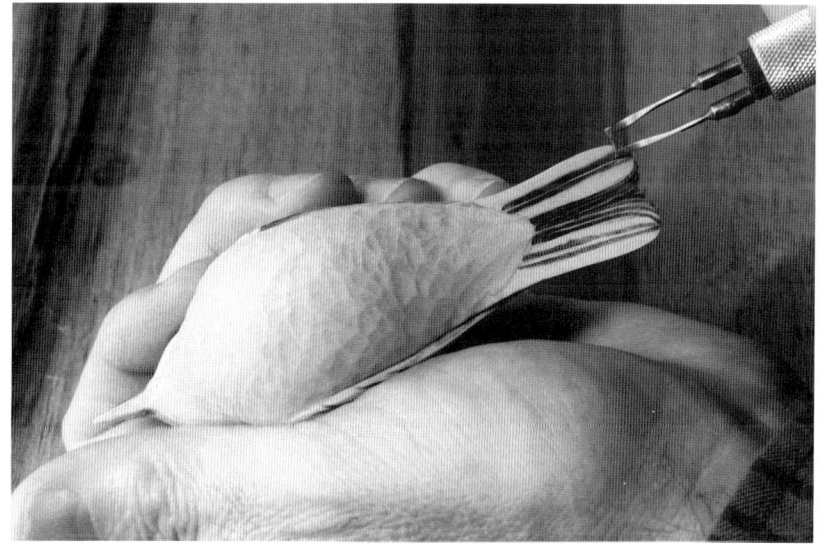

Turn the bird over and do the underside of the tail. Because of the way the feathers overlap on a bird's tail, the two outer feathers show the central shaft on the underside.

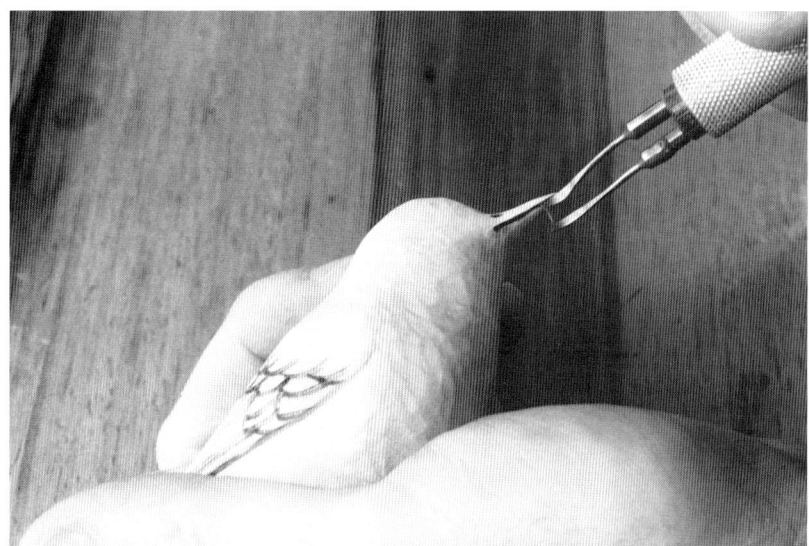

Very carefully burn-in a line showing the separation between the two halves of the beak.

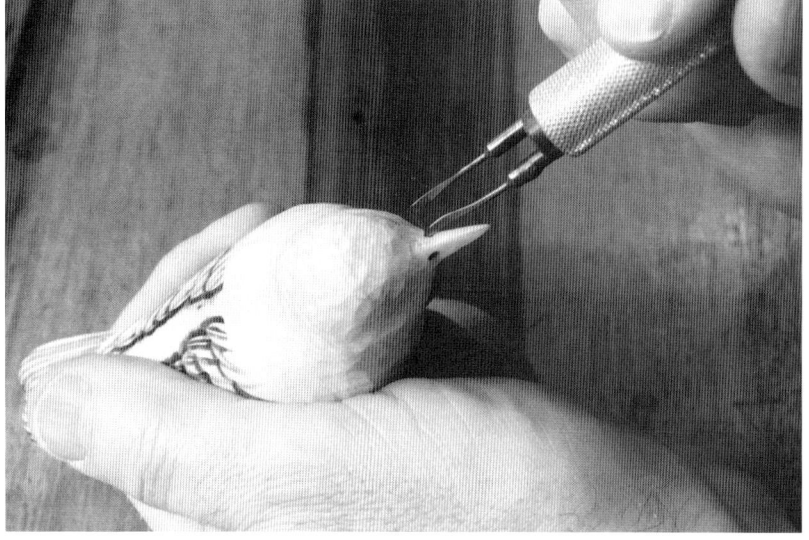

Use a corner of the tip to create a small hole for the nostril.

Next, look at the pattern and mark the position of the legs with pencil.

The easiest way I have found to hold a small songbird for painting is to use a holding stick made from scrap wood. Find a piece of wood about 6 inches long and about 1 inch across. Mine is made from a scrap of large dowel. Drill a hole in one end and glue the head of a wood screw, such as a 1½-inch-long no. 6, into it with epoxy putty. Let the putty harden thoroughly.

Make a starter hole with a scratch awl where one of the legs will be inserted and simply fasten the blackburnian warbler to the holding stick. A starter hole makes it easier to insert the screw and reduces the danger of splitting the wood.

I like to seal the carving with a light coat of spray lacquer before painting. This protects the wood and makes a better painting surface than raw wood. The type I use is Deft Semi-Gloss Clear Wood Finish in aerosol cans. For best results read all the instructions on the can first. Let the lacquer dry for at least thirty minutes before proceeding.

Spraying with lacquer may raise the grain slightly in the areas you have sanded. If the wood seems a little rough after the lacquer has dried, smooth it by sanding very lightly with 280 or finer grit sandpaper.

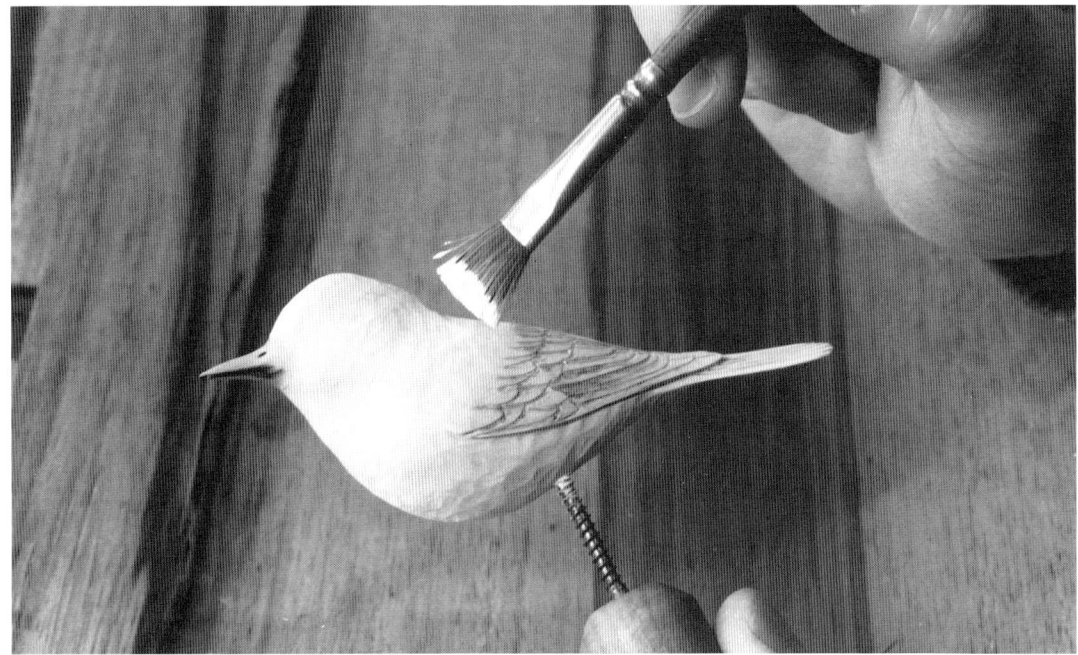

Then, brush a coat of white gesso paint on the entire carving except the beak. Use a fairly large, flat, synthetic sable brush, such as a no. 6, and apply the gesso in a smooth, even coat.

Next, texture the paint and even out any irregularities by first wiping your brush dry and then, starting at the tail, making light brush strokes in the direction of the feather barbs. That is, start from the center of the middle tail feather and lightly drag your brush diagonally toward the edges of the tail. This will create tiny ridges of texture that have the appearance of finely detailed feathers in the completed carving.

Do the same with the wing feathers. For the rest of the body, just make short finishing strokes with your paintbrush in the direction the smaller feathers lie. Then let the paint dry for a couple of hours.

The gesso provides a good surface for the paint to adhere to, and the white color ensures that your paint colors will not be affected by the underlying wood tones.

After the gesso has dried, you can insert the eyes. I apply the gesso first because it is difficult to clean off the glass eyes. I use clear glass eyes with a black pupil. This way I can paint the back of the eye the proper color for each species of bird. A good size for warbler eyes is 5mm.

Start by drawing small circles on the sides of the bird's head, marking the position of the eyes. Study the patterns closely for correct placement. Be particularly careful to check the position from the front, making sure the eyes are level. Also look down on the bird's head from the top and check that both eyes are the same distance from the beak. If the eyes are not in the same position on both sides of the head your bird will have a strange, "cockeyed" look.

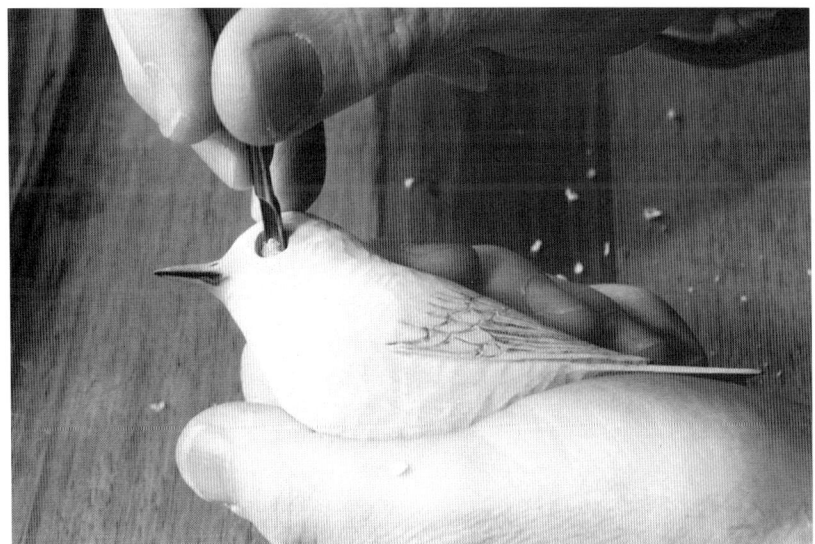

Carve a hole for the eye to fit into by making vertical cuts around the outside of the eye with a very small gouge, such as a 4mm no. 9. Then scoop out a hollow for the eye with the same gouge. Test-fit the eye in the hole as you work to make sure you get a good fit. The eye should slip in easily without a lot of extra room around it.

Blackburnian Warbler • 39

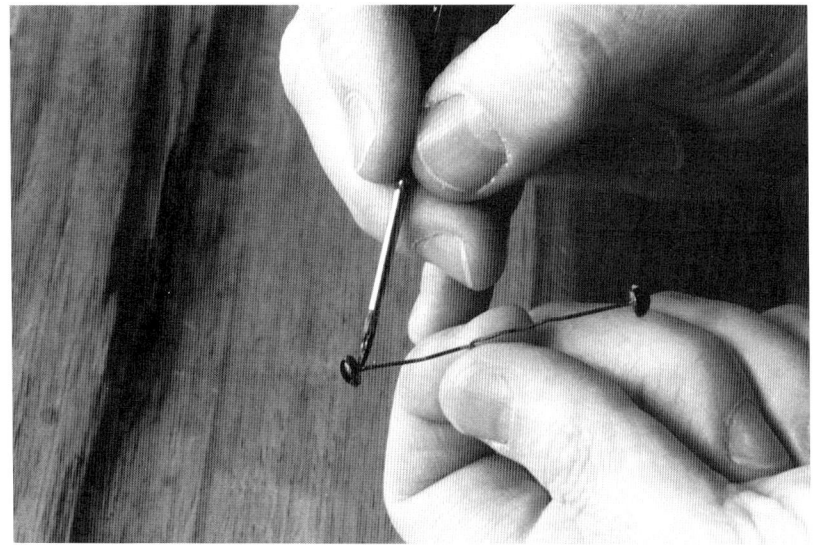

Paint the backs of the eyes brown with a mixture of burnt sienna and burnt umber acrylic. For a subtle sparkle, add a touch of thalo copper to the paint. Use a small, pointed brush, such as a no. 1 synthetic sable. Let the paint dry thoroughly.

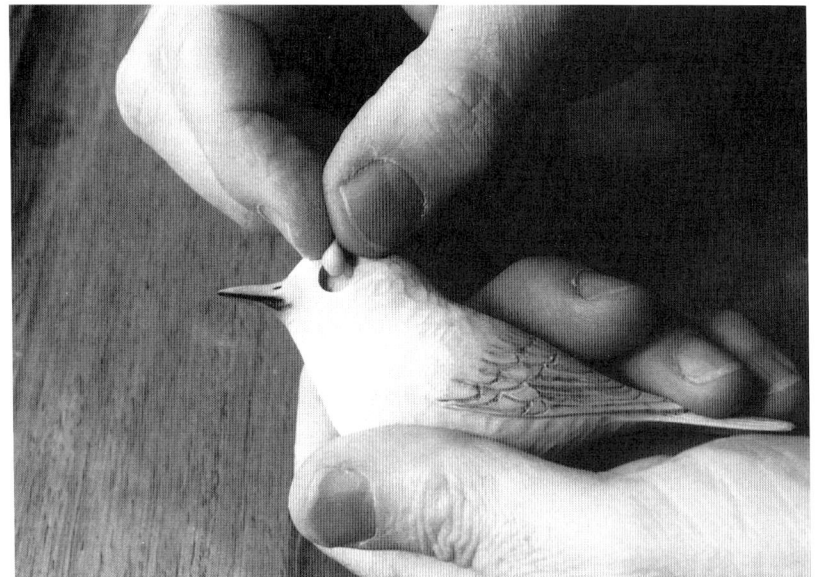

I use epoxy putty to set in the eyes. This is a compound with a claylike texture that comes in two parts that must be mixed together before use. Be sure to use equal portions of each part and mix thoroughly, or the putty will not harden properly.

Several brands of epoxy putty are on the market. I prefer the one sold by Brookstone. It hardens to a neutral gray color that blends with wood tones and takes paint well.

Form a bit of putty into a small ball and press it into the eye socket.

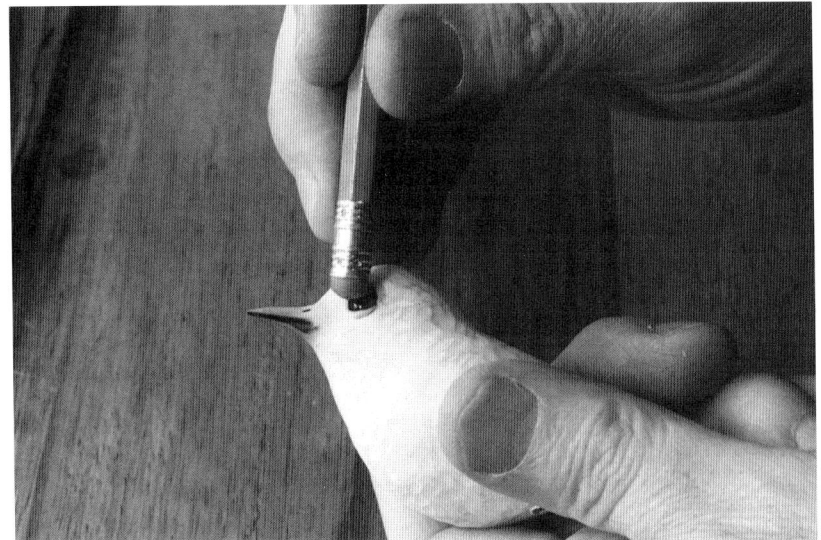

Then, gently press the glass eye down into the putty with the blunt end of a pencil or paintbrush. A small amount of putty will ooze out around the eye as you press it in. This excess putty is used to form the eyelid. You can adjust the amount of putty by adding or removing tiny bits.

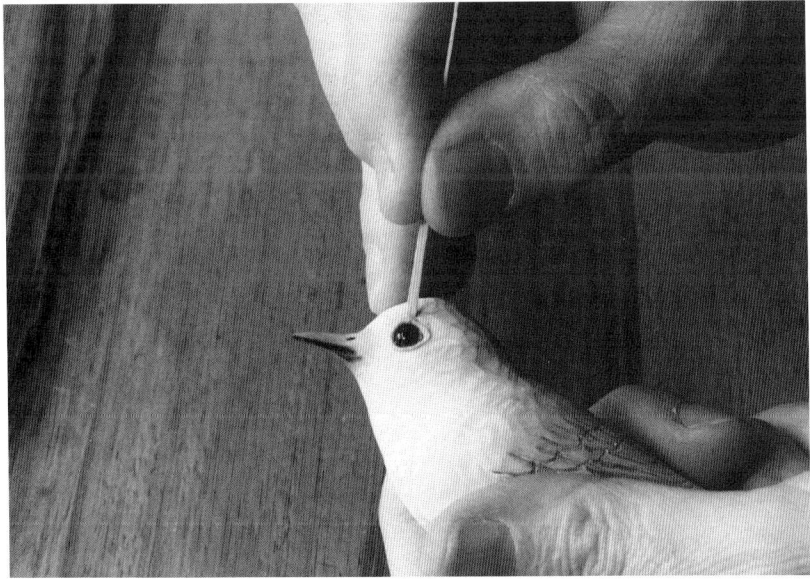

After the eye is inserted, use the flat end of a toothpick to shape the eyelid.

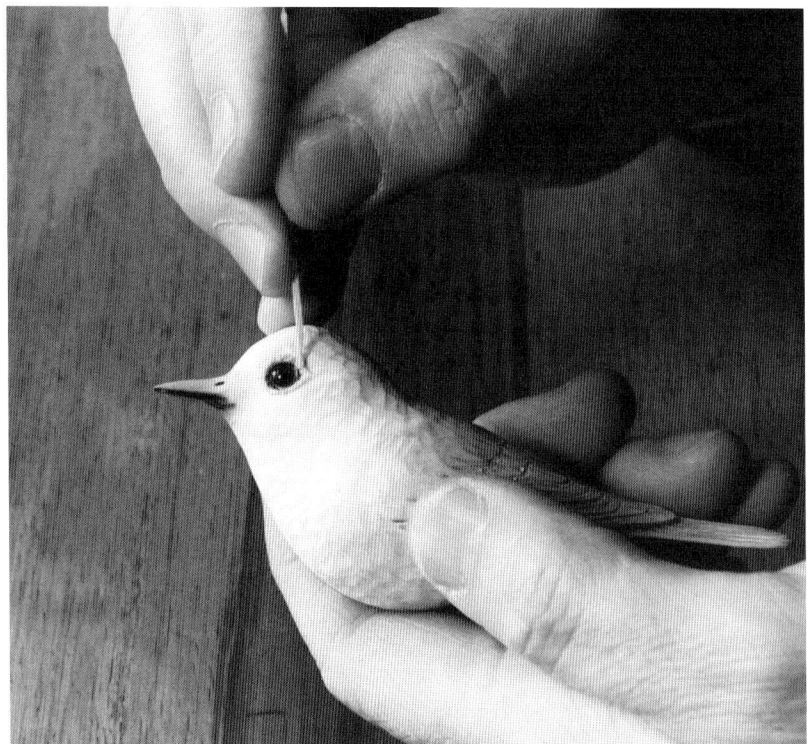

Then, texture the skin of the eyelid with the pointed end of the toothpick. If you like, you can whittle a finer point on the toothpick with your carving knife. If you have some good closeup photos of small songbirds, study them to get a feeling for the unique texture of a bird's eyelid. Compared with a mammal's eyelids, a bird's look almost beaded. Let the putty harden for at least two hours before beginning to paint.

PAINTING

For detailed instructions on painting the blackburnian warbler, please refer to the chapter on painting techniques.

MOUNTING

After the blackburnian warbler has been painted, it is ready to be mounted. Mounting is the final step and deserves as much time and thought as carving and painting. A good mount will always improve the appearance of a carving. Sloppy mounting will always detract, no matter how fine the carving itself.

There are as many different ways to mount songbirds as there are bird carvers. As you become more experienced, you will probably develop some special technique of your own. The method I use shows off the carvings in a simple, natural setting that enhances their beauty without competing with it.

The materials you need include a base, feet, and a stick to mount the bird on. I prefer small, round, black walnut bases. Black walnut has a beautiful grain, but the color is dark and subtle enough that it doesn't draw attention away from the carving. Bases 4 to 5 inches in diameter work well with these tiny birds.

You can make bases if you have the power tools for shaping wood, or you can buy finished bases in many different sizes and shapes from several suppliers.

A carved songbird's legs and feet should be made of metal. They are so thin that wooden legs would simply not be strong enough to support the weight of the carving. Some carvers make their own feet using wire and other materials. For larger carvings I often use this method, but for small songbirds, very accurately detailed cast metal feet are available. They are made of a pewter alloy that is flexible enough to be bent into realistic positions without breaking. I prefer the type with one small post at the top, which is inserted into the body, and another at the bottom, which goes into the branch the bird is mounted on.

All three of these warblers take the smallest size foot available. When I order feet, I usually get a few extra pairs to have on hand for my next carvings, and to have a spare in case I break one in the mounting process. This doesn't happen very often, but if it does, it can be frustrating waiting for new feet to arrive so that you can finish your carving.

Look at the feet carefully when they arrive. The two feet of a pair may look identical at first glance, but there are actually a right and a left foot. Often they are marked, but if not, the shortest of the three toes is always on the inside of the foot. Keep the individual pairs of feet separate; if you mix them all up together you might accidentally end up with a bird with two left feet.

Sometimes the feet have tiny tabs of metal flashing left on them from the casting process. If this is the case, simply trim them off with a sharp pocketknife. *Never* use your carving knife for this; it will dull or even notch the blade.

Finally, you need a stick for the bird to perch on. I prefer dry, dead branches without bark. Bark may crack and peel off the branch as it dries. If you live near water, you may find some small driftwood twigs to use. Otherwise, check your lawn after a windstorm. Often dead branches that have been blown out of the trees will be perfect for mounting carvings on.

For the easiest mounting, choose branches that have a twig coming off at a right angle from the main branch. Branches about $3/8$ inch to $1/2$ inch thick work best. Too thin a branch may break when you drill holes for the feet into it.

Other than those few suggestions, choose any branch that appeals to you. It all comes down to whatever branch you like best with your particular bird.

Before you begin mounting, lay out all your supplies and materials. In addition to the base, feet, and branch you will need a drill with an assortment of drill bits, and some quick-set epoxy glue.

Begin by painting a base coat of burnt umber acrylic on the legs and feet with a no. 2 or no. 4 flat brush. Do not paint the parts of the legs that will be glued into the bird and the branch. After the carving is mounted you will probably have to touch up the paint on the feet, as some may rub off during the mounting process.

While the legs and feet dry, drill a hole in the base the same size or slightly smaller than the branch you are going to use. Test-fit the branch in the hole. If necessary you can adjust the branch's shape with your carving knife for a good fit. Glue the stick into the base with quick-set epoxy glue.

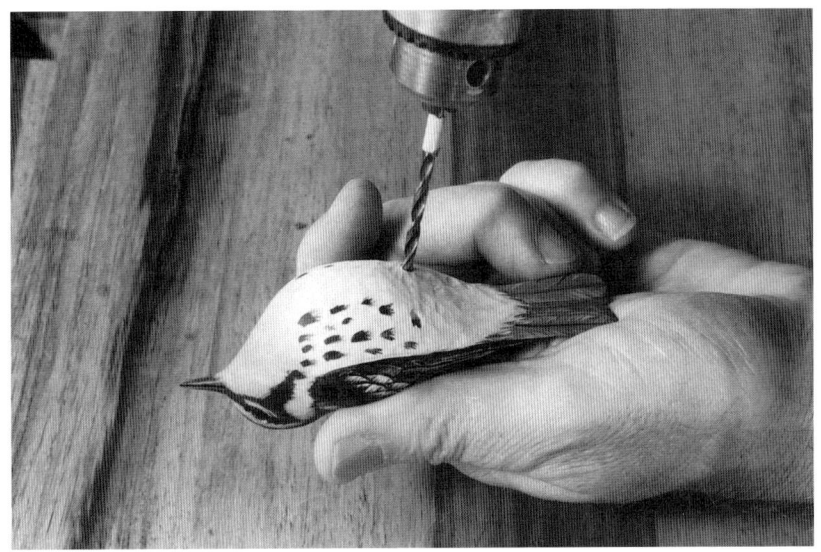

Then use a drill bit the same thickness as the part of the leg that extends into the body to drill leg holes in the bird. I used a 1/8-inch drill bit on these. Be sure to make a starter hole with a scratch awl before you drill so that the drill bit doesn't wander. Use a sharp drill bit and work slowly. Don't put too much pressure on the wood; let the drill bit do the cutting to avoid splitting the wood.

If the drill does splinter the wood around the opening for the leg a little, don't worry. You can patch it with a tiny piece of epoxy putty and touch up the paint after the carving is mounted.

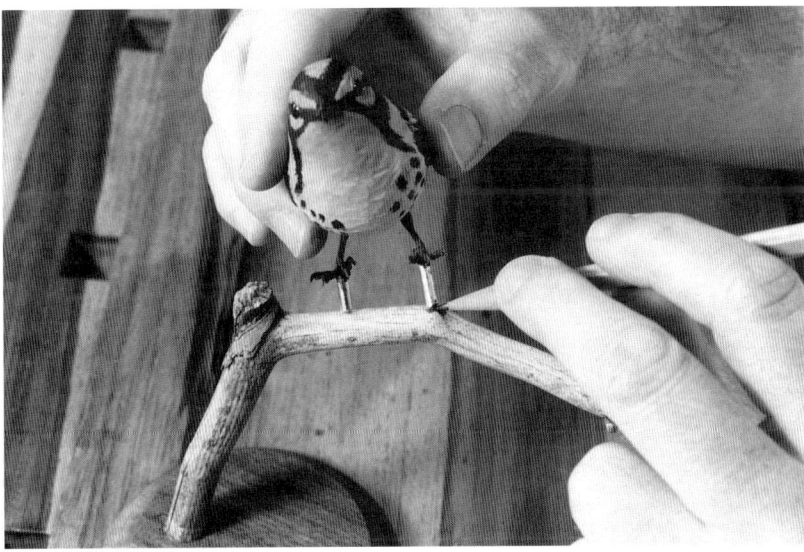

Test-fit the legs in the holes. They should slip in easily without a lot of extra room. When you are happy with the way the legs fit into the body, hold the carving on the branch and mark where to drill the holes for the feet.

Blackburnian Warbler • 45

Make starter holes with a scratch awl and drill the holes carefully into the branch. Once again, work slowly and let the drill bit do the cutting.

Test-fit the bird on the branch. You may find you need to make the holes in the branch a little deeper. Or, if your branch is thin, you can trim the posts on the bottoms of the bird's feet a little shorter with wire cutters.

At this point you can bend the legs slightly so the bird sits in a natural position. You can also bend the toes down a little, but don't wrap them around the branch yet.

If you are feeling brave, you can go ahead and glue the entire thing together now, gluing the legs into the body and onto the branch in one step.

Or, you can do it in two stages. First, mix a little quick-set epoxy. Put some in the holes in the body and some on the top part of the legs using a toothpick to apply it. Insert the legs into the body, then dry-fit the bird onto the branch and hold the carving in place until the glue sets. Holding the bird on the branch ensures that the legs harden in the body in the right position.

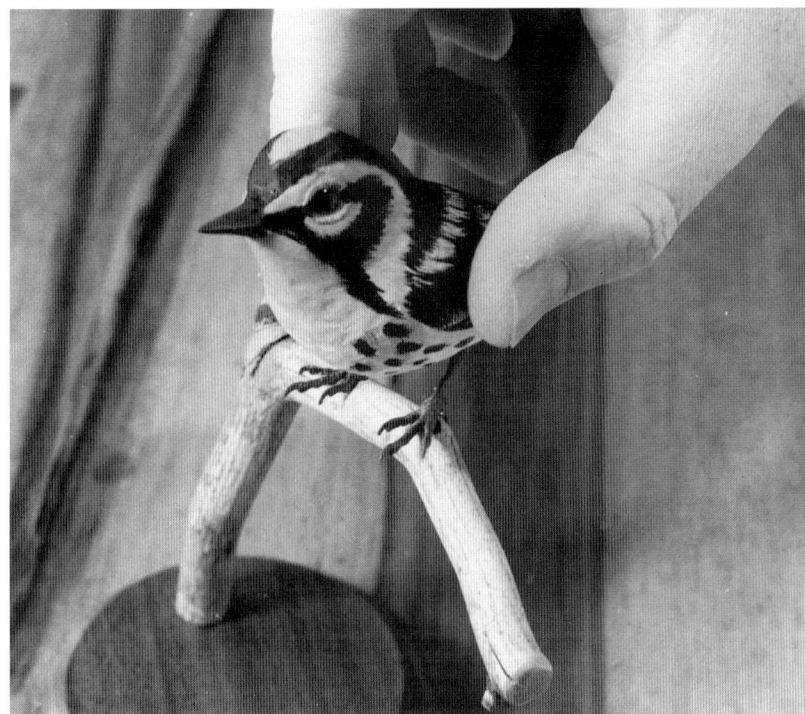

Then, when the glue has hardened, mix a fresh batch of epoxy and glue the bird to the branch. Once again, hold it in place until the glue sets.

Let the glue cure. Although quick-set epoxy hardens in a few minutes, it does not develop full strength for several hours.

After the glue has cured, very gently bend the toes around the branch. Do this very slowly and gradually. A bird usually holds a branch rather loosely; the tip of each claw does not have to dig into the wood.

When the bird is securely glued to the branch, you can make any final adjustments to the angles of the legs and the positions of the toes.

Blackburnian Warbler

Once the bird is mounted, touch up any chipped paint on the feet, or any glue spots where the legs go into the body with acrylic paint using a tiny, pointed sable brush.

Magnolia Warbler

Magnolia warblers (*Dendroica magnolia*) live at a middle height in the forest. I often sit on the front porch with my coffee and watch one as he works his way along the edge of the woods next to my home. He is a beautiful warbler with a distinctive white, black, and blue-gray head. Most striking, though, is the bright yellow breast spotted with black.

The male of each species of warbler has a different song, which he sings loudly in the spring. I always listen for the magnolia's song so I'll know when he is back from his long trip south. To me it sounds like "dee-dee-dee, dee-oh." As soon as I hear it I get out my binoculars and go looking for him.

The best time to see warblers is in the early spring before the trees leaf out. These birds are so small that they can hide behind a single leaf later in the season.

This bird is carved in a typical warbler position, with the wings and tail fanned slightly. In making this carving you will learn how to detail the wings and tail, and how to carve the turned head. This pose gives your warbler an alert and lively look. I will also show you a new wet-on-wet painting technique that brings out all the subtle beauty of the magnolia warbler's coloring.

For the magnolia warbler, choose a piece of

basswood without knots or deformities in the grain. I like basswood for small songbirds because it has a fine, even grain and resists splitting. This is especially important for the magnolia warbler, with its delicate dropped wing tips. Also, because the head is turned, the grain runs diagonally in the beak, making it more fragile. Basswood's resistance to splitting is a real asset in such a situation.

MAGNOLIA WARBLER

Tools

Carving knife
8mm no. 12 V-gouge
8mm no. 5 bent gouge
3mm no. 12 V-gouge
4mm no. 9 gouge
Woodburning pen with 4-C tip
Drill and bits
Paintbrushes

Materials

Basswood:
    5 inches by 2 inches by 1¾ inches
4-inch walnut base
1 pair 5mm clear glass eyes
1 pair small cast pewter legs
Spray lacquer
Epoxy putty
Quick-set epoxy glue
280-grit sandpaper
Gesso
Alkyd paints
    ultramarine blue
    burnt umber
    titanium white
    ivory black
    cadmium yellow light
Acrylic paints
    titanium white
    ultramarine blue
    burnt umber
    ivory black

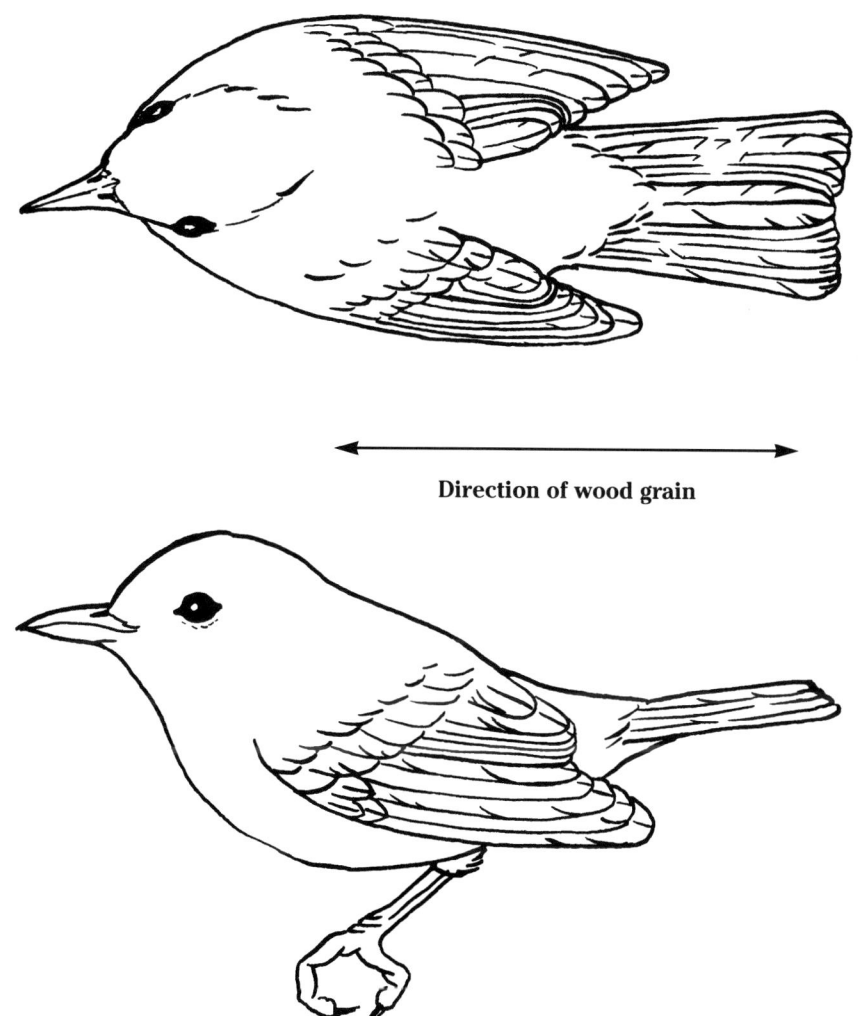

Direction of wood grain

Begin with a block of wood about 5 inches long by 2 inches wide by 1¾ inches thick. Be sure the grain runs lengthwise for strength. Trace the profile of the magnolia warbler on the wood with a pencil.

Next, use a band saw or coping saw to cut along the outline.

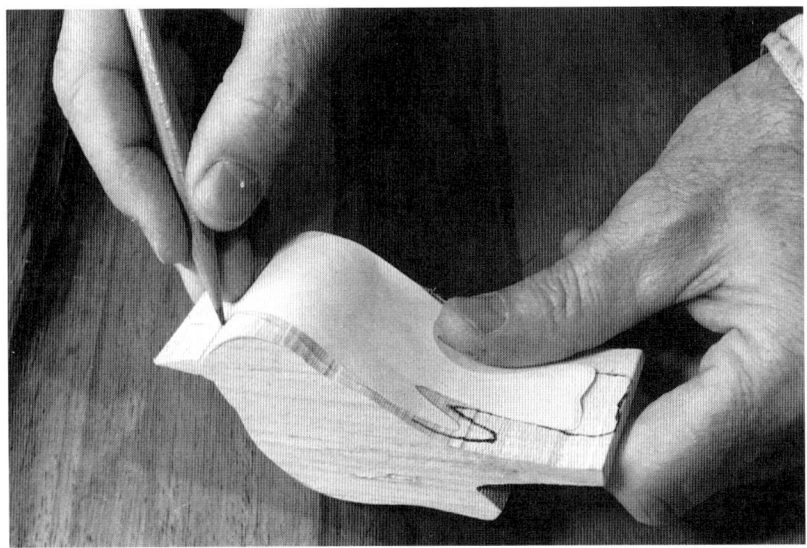

Then, trace the top pattern on the blank. I suggest lining up the tail section, tracing the tail and wing tips, then sliding the pattern forward to trace the beak and head. It works best this way because the blank is curved but the pattern is flat.

Start by using a carving knife with a short, straight blade about 1¼ inches long to narrow the sides of the head and beak while viewing the bird from above.

Watch the direction of the wood grain around the beak carefully. It might be necessary to carve toward the tip of the beak on the right side of the head and toward the body on the left to avoid going against the grain. Just be aware of this possibility as you carve, and if you feel the knife start to dig into the wood as you make a cut, try carving from the opposite direction. For more information on working with the grain, refer to Getting Started.

Don't make the beak too thin or pointed at this time; leave a little extra wood. The final shaping will be done later.

Draw lines on each side of the blank to indicate the edges of the wings.

Next, round the abdomen below the wings.

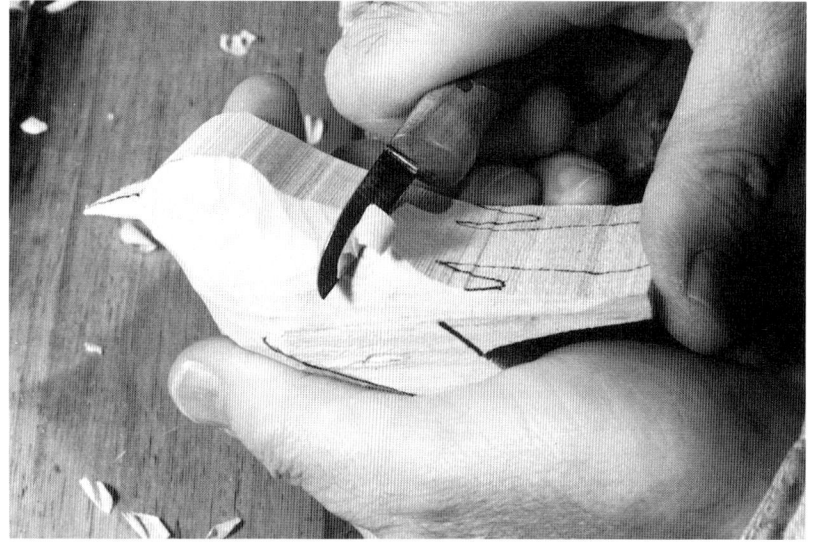

Then, round the corners of the back and the back of the neck. These steps remove some of the excess wood on the blank before you begin shaping the tail section.

Redraw the lines for the top edge of the wing. I often carve off and redraw the guidelines several times in the process of making a carving.

Now, cut a notch narrowing the sides of the tail. Do not remove the wood right up to the guidelines marking the top edge of the wing. Leave a little excess, as this area will be detailed later. I recommend removing the wood in two or three stages rather than trying to cut it all out at once.

After the tail is narrowed, draw guidelines on the underside of the bird to show where the wing tips extend beyond the sides of the abdomen and the abdomen narrows to the base of the tail. The abdomen is about 1½ inches wide at the widest part.

Then, remove the excess wood between the wing tips down to the base of the tail so that the shapes flow smoothly from the abdomen to the underside of the tail. The best way to do this is to start with a small notch in the center.

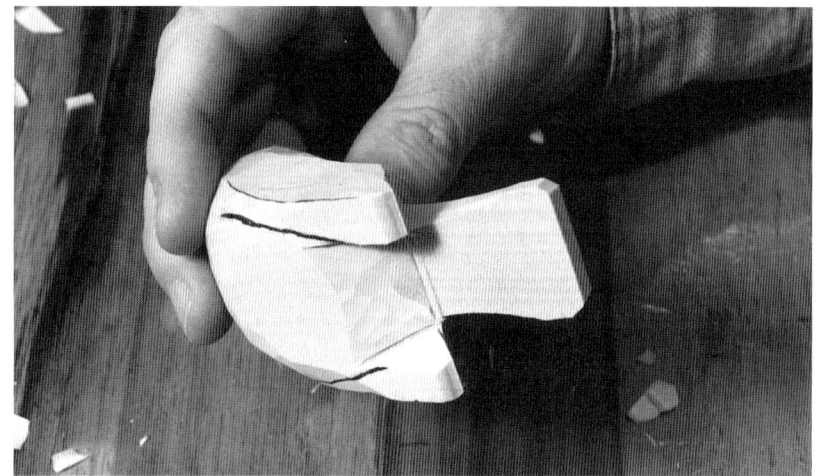

Continue removing wood by widening and deepening the notch until the lower abdomen is level with the tail.

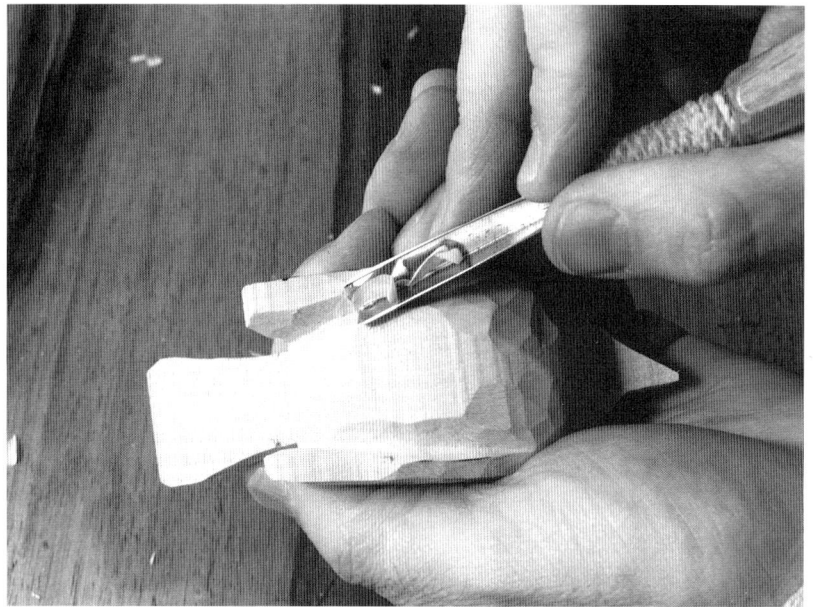

Next, use a medium-size V-gouge, such as an 8mm no. 12, to incise a notch between the abdomen and the wings. This step allows you to round the abdomen and shape the wing tips.

Notice that I am holding the gouge in the pencil grip with the fingers of both hands braced on the wood for safety and control. The hand holding the carving is also positioned out of the path of the tool in case it slips. If you have not used gouges on a small, handheld carving before, refer to Getting Started for complete instructions.

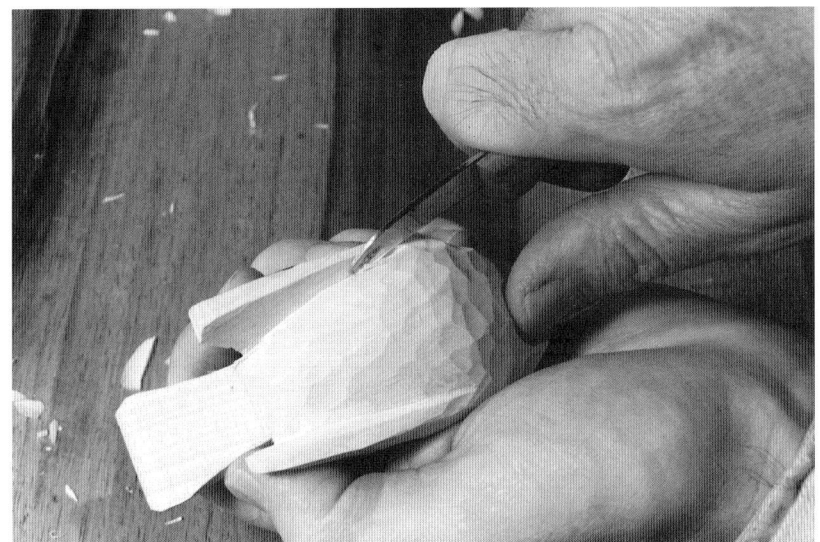

Use the knife to round the abdomen and smooth the inner surfaces of the wings. This step establishes the distance between the wing tips. On my bird the distance between the inner surfaces of the wing tips is 1¼ inches, but this can vary slightly from carving to carving. Take your time with this step and watch the grain direction carefully to avoid splintering.

Smooth the underside of the tail, hollowing it out slightly with an 8mm no. 5 gouge. I find that a bent gouge, which has a curved shaft, is very handy for this step because it fits around the curved shape of the abdomen better than a straight gouge.

Now that the basic shapes are established on the underside of the bird, you can start shaping the back. Thin the outside of the wings down, curving the tips in slightly. Take your time with this step. The wing tips are fragile, so it is best to remove the wood in small, thin shavings. Since the delicately curved wings are important in recreating the graceful beauty of a magnolia warbler, it is a step worth the extra time it takes.

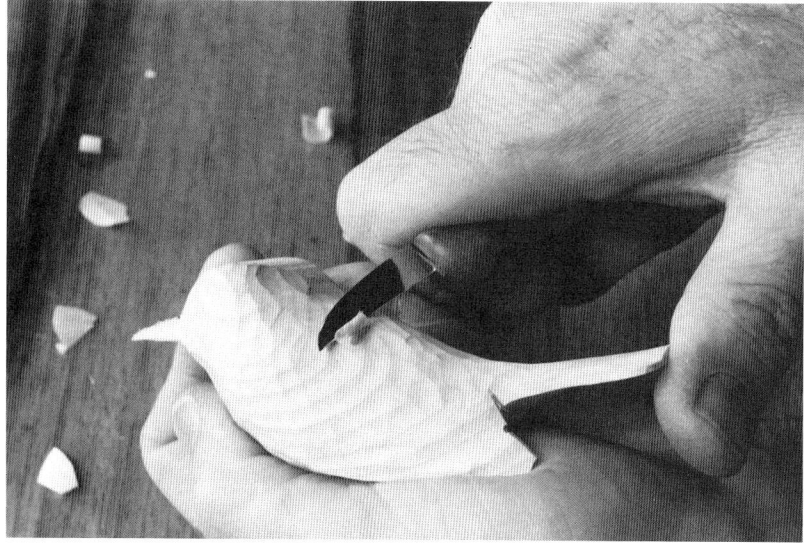

Smooth and round the upper surface of the wings and back.

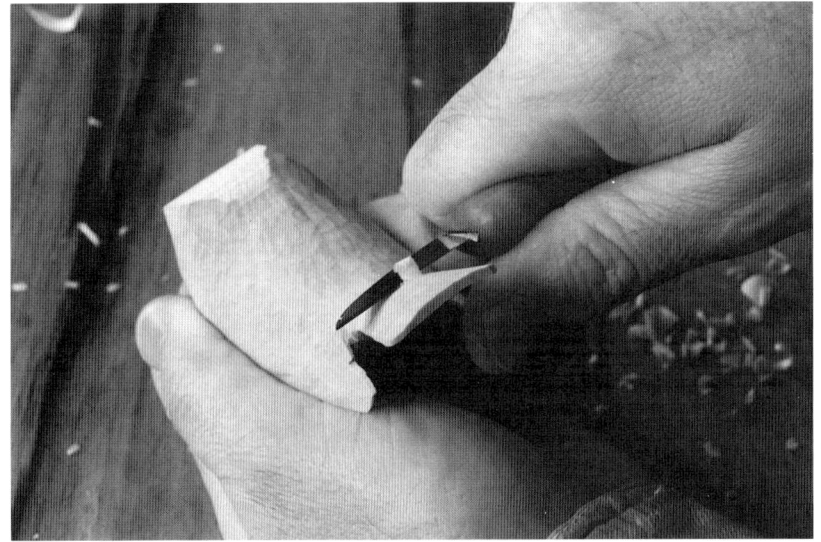

Round the upper surface of the tail. A bird's tail is not perfectly flat but has a slight curve from side to side. Be alert for changes in the grain as you work.

Don't make the tail too thin. You can create the illusion of delicacy and lightness by the way you shape the edges, leaving the center portion thicker for strength. At this point the tail should be about $1/8$ inch thick in the center and about $1/16$ inch thick at the edges. This leaves enough wood at the edges for the final shaping, which will be done later.

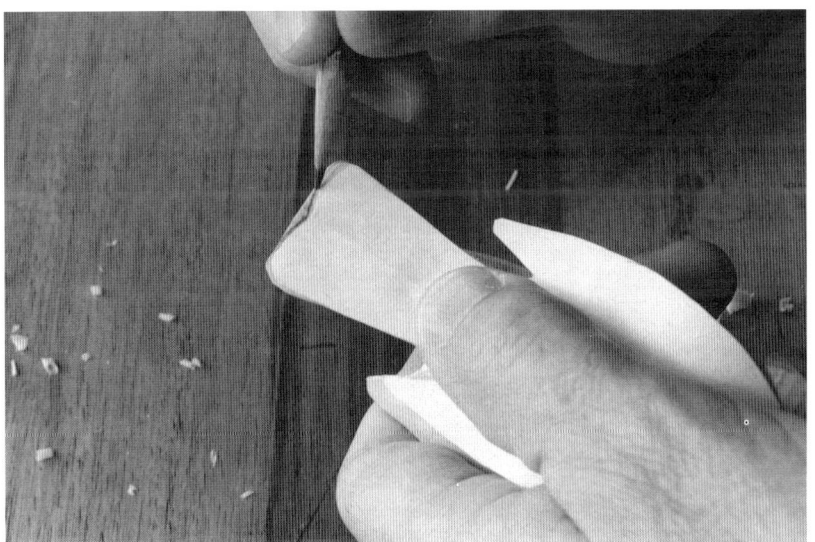

Next, place the pattern for the top view on the tail and sketch in the notch at the tip. Note that the tail is only slightly notched. A warbler's tail does not have a deep fork, and the notch is even less noticeable when the tail is fanned.

Cut the notch out with the carving knife. Make sure your knife is razor sharp; you are cutting across the grain, and a dull knife will crush and tear the wood.

Now, remove paper-thin shavings from the tail to thin the edges. I find it easiest to thin from the top side.

After the tail is shaped, pencil in a line showing the rear edge of the wing tips.

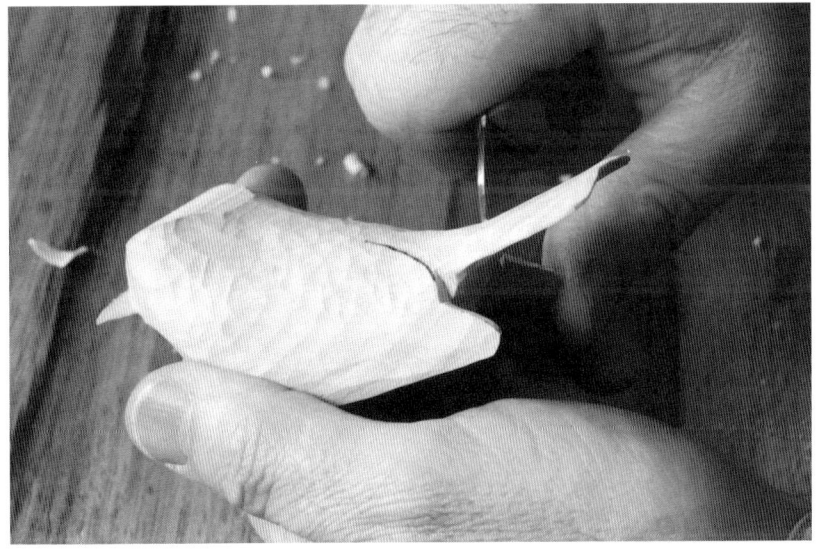

Use your knife to do the final shaping of the wing edge following the outlines. Notice that the wing tips are still thick at this point.

Magnolia Warbler • **63**

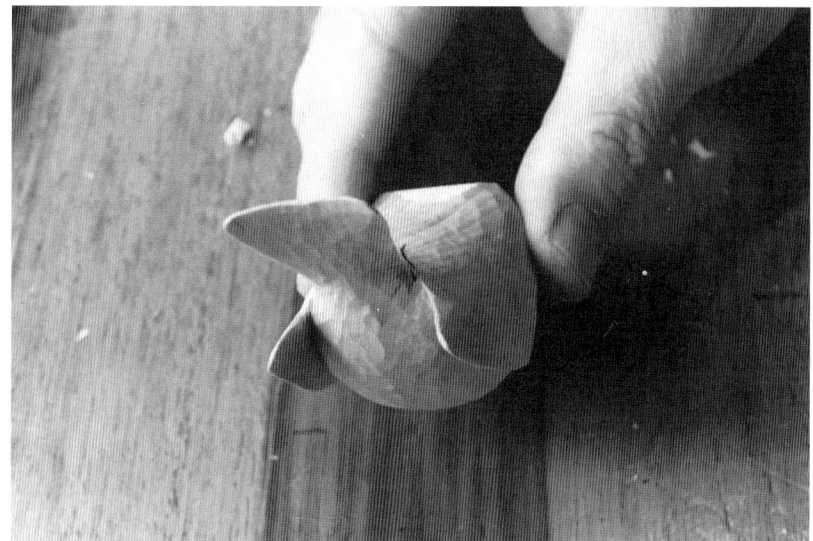

Thin the wing tips with the carving knife, but don't make them too thin and fragile. You can do a final shaping with fine sandpaper when the carving is done. Never use sandpaper on a carving until you are completely done using the knife and carving gouges, however. Tiny bits of abrasive from the sandpaper embedded in the grain will dull your knife.

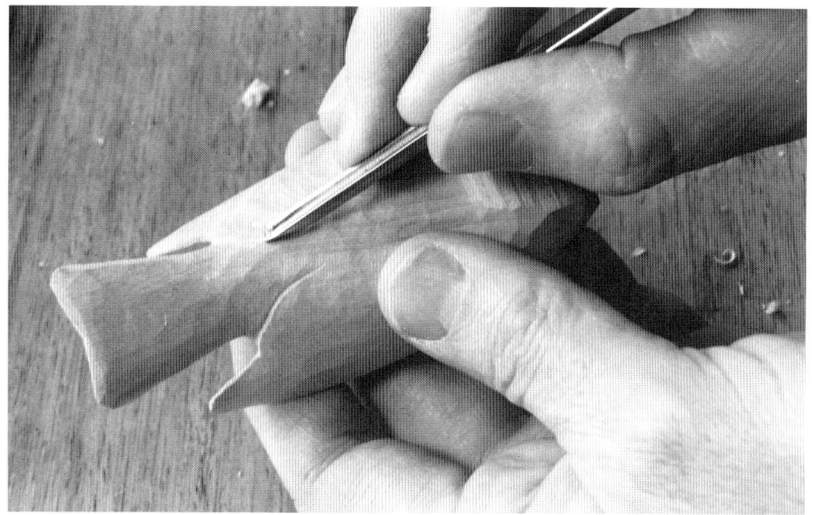

Then use a small V-gouge, such as a 3mm no. 12, to incise a very shallow groove on the back, separating the wing edge from the body.

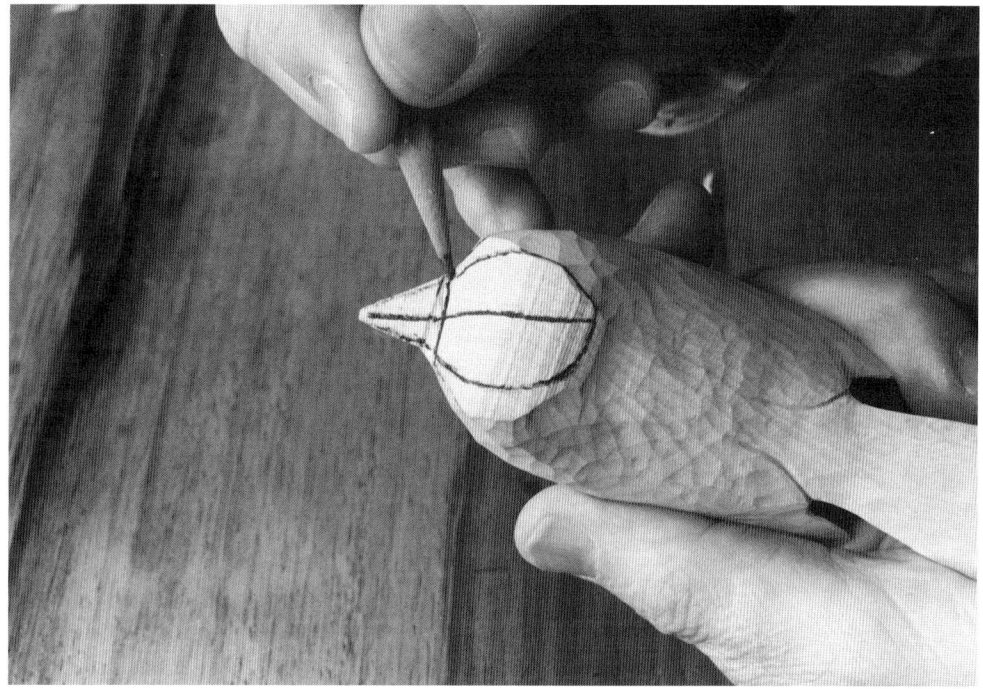

After the tail and wings are shaped, you can move on to the head. The magnolia warbler has a turned head that enhances the lifelike quality of the carving by making it look more alert and lively. Carving the turned head is not difficult, but it can be tricky to visualize the shapes you want. I have developed a few techniques I think you will find helpful when you carve any small songbirds with turned heads.

Begin by drawing some guidelines on the top of the head. Start with a centerline that runs the length of the beak and the top of the head. Then draw curved lines to indicate the sides of the head. Finally, draw a short line perpendicular to the centerline to indicate the base of the beak.

These guidelines will help you shape the head symmetrically. Also—and this is very important—they will help you make sure that the beak and head are pointing in the same direction. You don't want a beak that looks crooked.

Then, viewing the carving from the top, thin the neck and head to match the lines you have drawn. I find it works best to carve upward from the shoulder toward the top of the head. Working in this direction creates a smooth, flowing shape reflecting the sleek curves of a living warbler.

After the head and neck are thinned down, look at the carving from the front and round the top of the head. Do not round the beak at this point.

Next, look from the side—the profile view—and adjust the shapes of the head, neck, and beak.

This method of shaping the head by looking at one view at a time—top, front, and side—is very useful for carving the head of any bird or animal.

Look at the carving from the top once again and adjust the shape of the beak. For a carving whose head is turned I save this step until last because the beak is so delicate. Make the beak slender and tapering. It is the same size as the blackburnian warbler's, about $17/32$ inch long and $7/32$ inch wide at the base. At this point the beak is still square in cross section.

If you like, you can draw a guideline down the center of the beak looking from the top, or you can carve it freehand. Shape the beak the same way you did the blackburnian warbler's, creating a somewhat triangular upper half and a rounded lower half.

For a final detail you can carve some very shallow hollows on the side of the head: one where the eye will be set in and one below that to suggest the patch of feathers called the ear coverts. I use my carving knife, removing the wood in tiny chips that are so thin they are nearly transparent. You can also use a gouge; the 8mm no. 5 mentioned earlier will work, but a gouge with a greater sweep, or more curvature on the cutting edge, such as an 8mm or 10mm no. 9, will be easier to use. This is a very delicate step, so use a light hand and remove only a little wood at a time.

Now the actual carving process is completed. I recommend sanding the carving lightly with fine 280-grit aluminum oxide or garnet paper. I sand the areas where I will be burning-in the feather texture—the wings and both top and underside of the tail—quite smooth. This ensures that the woodburned line will look straight and even.

The rest of the bird is sanded only enough to mellow the tool marks but not obscure them completely. After the carving is painted, the subtle shapes of these tool marks will suggest feather texture.

Look at the pattern for the magnolia warbler and sketch the wing and tail feathers on your carving. Don't try to draw the lines with mathematical precision. Too straight and even an arrangement of feathers will make your carving look stiff and unnatural, since the feathers on a live bird are never perfectly arranged.

Begin by burning-in the wing feathers with a 4-C tip. I like to start at the top of the wing with the coverts and work my way down to the primaries.

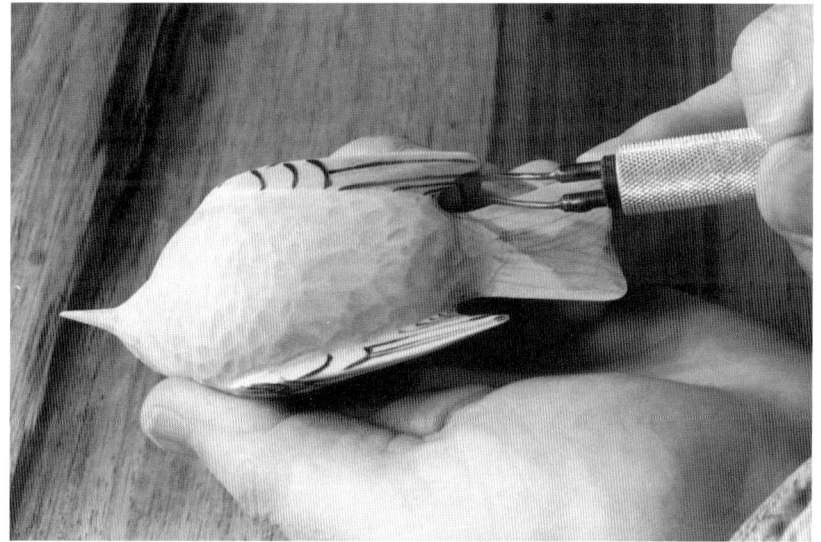

Because the magnolia warbler's wings are fanned out, you should burn-in the primary feathers on the underside of the wings as well.

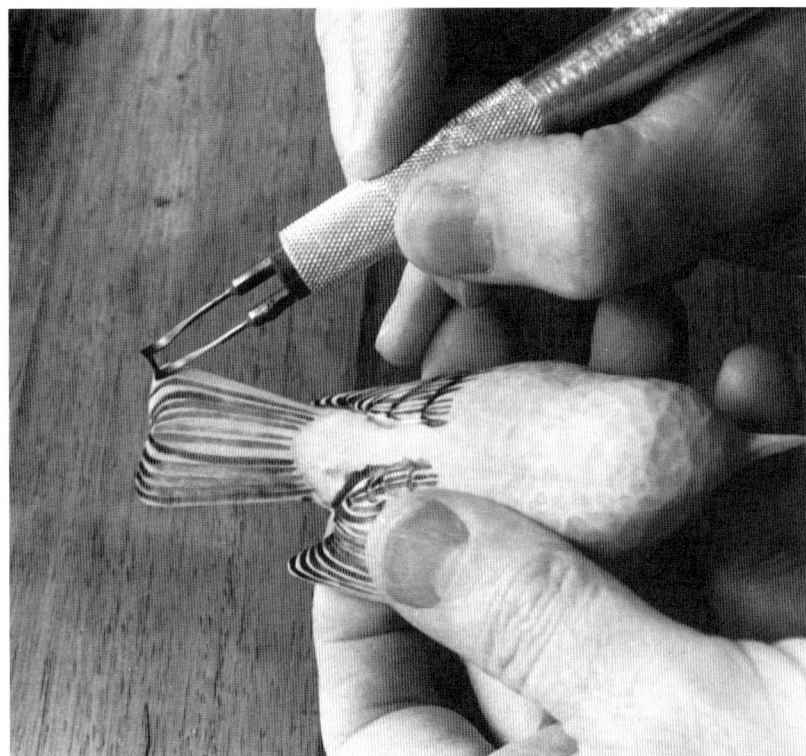

As a natural history note, a warbler has twelve tail feathers. Don't worry about trying to draw them all in. On both the tail and wings the feathers overlap, so they are seldom all visible at any one time. Just make sure you don't draw *more* than twelve feathers on the tail.

Burn-in the feathers on the top of the tail.

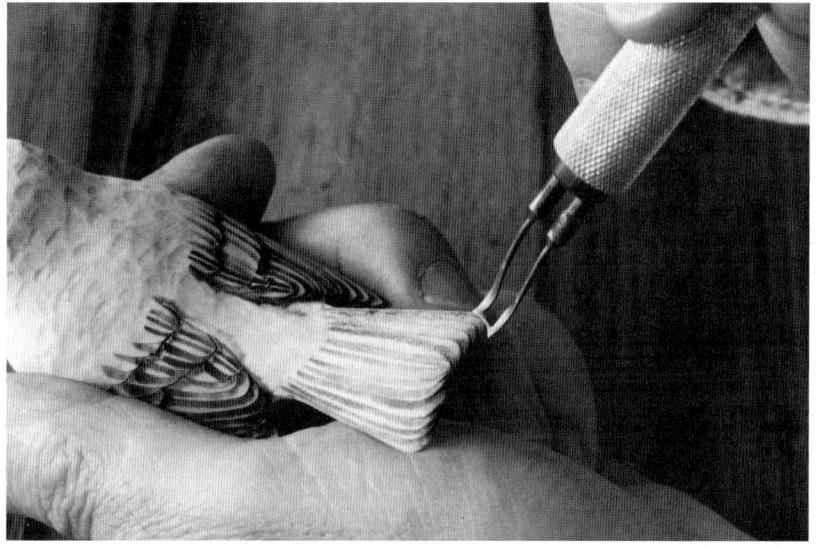

Because the magnolia warbler's tail feathers are fanned out, there is more separation between them at the tips. To create this effect, I use a modified 4-C woodburning tip made by filing a concave curve across the end with a small, fine, circular file. The sharper angle at the two corners of the tip makes it easier to burn-in fine details. Also, the curved inner portion allows you to create the separation between feathers, such as the tail feathers and the primary feathers at the wing tips.

This separation gives the effect of realistic overlapping feathers, and on the tail feathers it gives you a guide for sketching in the feather arrangement on the underside.

Next, burn-in the feathers on the underside of the tail. As an optional touch you can burn-in some breaks on the wing and tail feathers.

Use the same tip to burn-in a line showing the separation between the upper and lower mandibles.

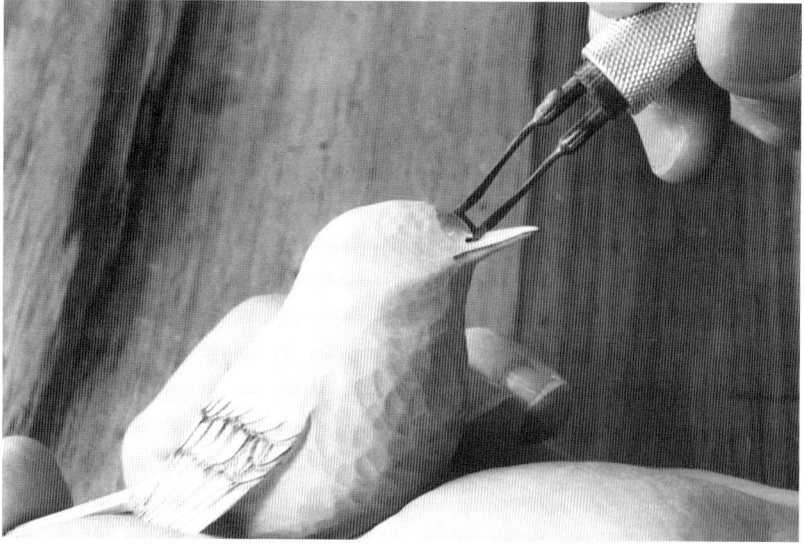

Finally, burn-in each nostril.

To make it easier to hold the bird for undercoating and painting, screw it to a holding stick.

After the bird is burned-in, I like to seal the carving with a light coat of spray lacquer the same way as on the blackburnian warbler.

When the lacquer is dry, brush a thin, even coat of white gesso on the whole carving except the beak. This is the same type of material used to prime artist's canvases because it provides a good surface for the paint to adhere to. A white undercoat ensures that your feather colors won't be affected by the underlying wood tones. Be sure to brush the gesso on in the same direction the feather barbs grow.

While the white undercoat is drying, paint the backs of a set of 5mm clear glass eyes brown with burnt umber acrylic and set them aside to dry.

Mark the position of the eyes on the carving, then carve a small hole for each eye to fit into with a tiny gouge, such as a 4mm no. 9. Test-fit the eye occasionally as you work. You want a hole that the eye will slip into easily without a lot of extra room.

The magnolia warbler's eyes are inserted exactly the same way as the blackburnian's. I recommend using epoxy putty to set the eyes in. Mix the two parts thoroughly so that the putty will harden properly.

Begin by forming a bit of putty into a small ball and pressing it into the eye socket. Then, gently press the eye down into the putty. I find the eraser end of a pencil is handy for this step. A little bit of putty will ooze out around the eye as you press it in. This can be used to form a realistic eyelid.

A toothpick is perfect for shaping the eyelids. Moisten the ends of it to keep the putty from sticking. Use the flat end of the toothpick to shape the eyelid. Then use the pointed end to texture the eyelid. Let the putty harden for a few hours before you go on.

PAINTING

For detailed instructions on painting the magnolia warbler, please refer to the chapter on painting techniques.

MOUNTING

The magnolia warbler is mounted exactly the same way as the blackburnian.

Paint a pair of legs dark brown with burnt umber acrylic. Be sure to leave the posts at the top and bottom unpainted so that the glue will adhere better.

While the paint dries, make a mount for the bird by drilling a hole in a walnut base and gluing a small branch into it.

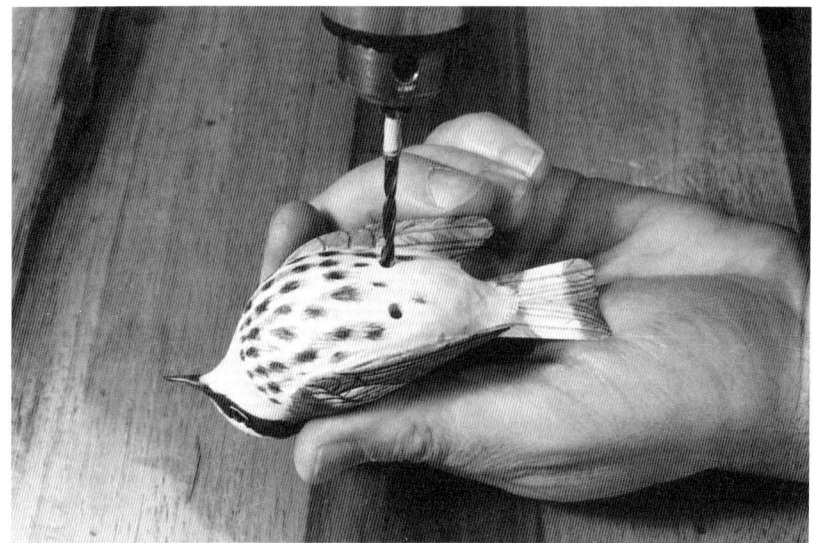

Then, make starter holes with a scratch awl on the underside of the warbler where the legs will be positioned. Drill a hole into the body with a bit that is the same size as the leg; mine was 1/8 inch in diameter. Drill carefully and don't put too much pressure on the wood; let the drill bit do the cutting.

Test-fit the legs into the body; they should slip in easily. Then, hold the carving up to the base you have made and mark the position for the holes in the branch. Carefully drill holes in the branch for the feet.

When you are sure the pieces fit together properly, glue the legs into the bird and the bird to the branch. As discussed in the blackburnian warbler chapter, you can do this in one step or two.

If you choose to assemble the pieces in two steps, first glue the legs into the bird. Hold it in position on the base while the glue sets to be sure the legs harden at the right angle. Then glue the bird to the base, once again holding it in position while the glue sets. Let the glue cure for several hours, or overnight for maximum strength.

When the quick-set epoxy glue has cured, adjust the position of the bird on the branch by gently bending the legs a little. Then, very carefully bend the toes so that they wrap around the branch in a realistic manner. They do not need to hold the branch in a death grip.

After you have made all the adjustments and the bird is in its final position, do any necessary touchup painting on the feet or body with acrylic paint and a tiny, pointed sable brush, such as a no. 0.

Parula Warbler

ALL WARBLERS ARE A PLEASURE TO WATCH, BUT THE parula *(Parula americana),* with delicately shaded colors, is special. Although parulas are not actually rare, they are elusive. I have seldom seen one singing loudly from a conspicuous perch the way a blackburnian or magnolia does. Instead, they flit about in the soft, filtered half-light of the forest understory like a kind of wood sprite.

They prefer habitats with plenty of moss and lichen for their nests. In southern woods, they nest in hanging clumps of Spanish moss.

I remember the first time I saw a parula warbler. It was feeding its family of three half-grown, fluffy chicks in a thicket along the path to a nearby pond. Every time I pass the spot I can't help looking to see if it's back.

The beautiful soft blue and yellow-orange coloring is an enjoyable challenge to paint. With this project I will show you some techniques for blending colors right on the bird to capture its beauty.

I have carved this parula warbler in a free-flying position—that is, as if it were actually in a moment of flight. I used a thin wire glued inside a tail feather to secure it to the branch. This technique is not as difficult as it looks, and once you have mastered it, you can use it for other flying

birds. I have used this method to display carved birds ranging in size from a tiny hummingbird to a bald eagle with a 3-foot wingspan.

If you prefer, however, you can mount this warbler in a perching position with the wings outstretched or folded close to the body like the blackburnian and the magnolia.

PARULA WARBLER

Tools

Carving knife
8mm no. 5 bent gouge
6mm no. 9 gouge
12mm no. 7 gouge
4mm no. 9 gouge
Woodburning pen with 4-C tip
Wire cutters
Pin vise
Drill and bits
Paintbrushes

Materials

3 blocks basswood:
    1 piece 4½ inches by 2 inches by 1½ inches
    2 pieces each 4 inches by 2 inches by ½ inch
Clear nail polish
18 gauge copper wire
4- or 5-inch walnut base
1 pair 5mm clear glass eyes
1 pair small cast pewter legs
Spray lacquer
Epoxy putty
Quick-set epoxy glue
280-grit sandpaper
Alkyd paints
    titanium white
    burnt umber
    cerulean blue
    ultramarine blue
    yellow ochre
    cadmium yellow light
    cadmium yellow medium
    cadmium red medium
    ivory black
    burnt sienna
Acrylic paints
    burnt umber
    ultramarine blue
    titanium white
    cerulean blue
    yellow orange
    orange red
    yellow ochre light

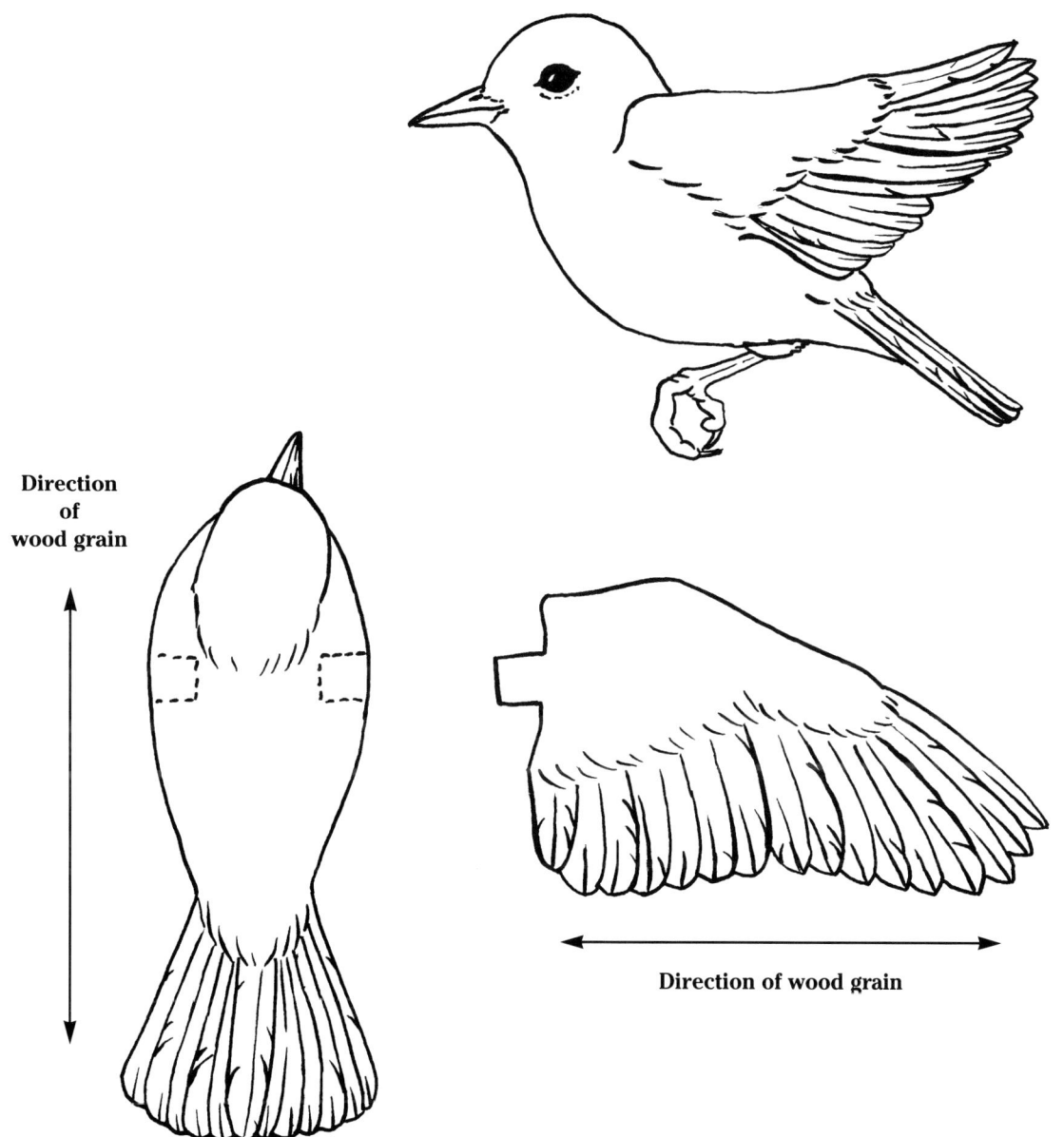

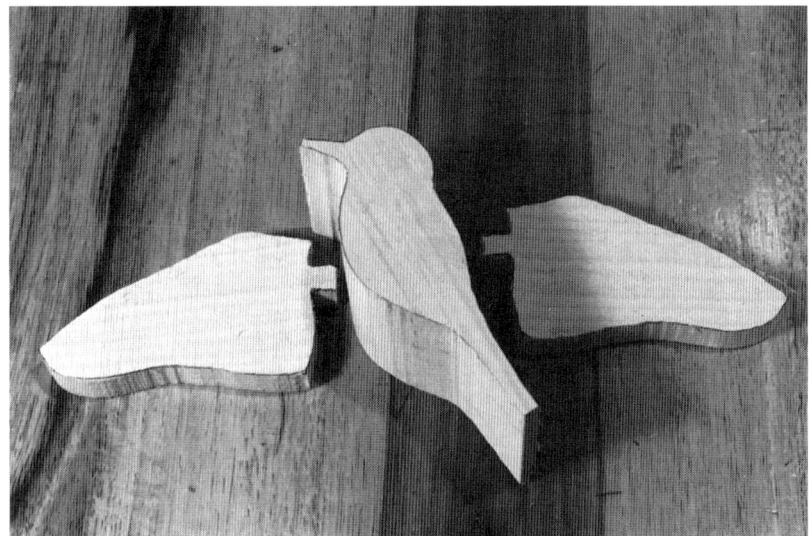

To carve the parula warbler you will need one block of basswood 4½ inches long by 2 inches wide by 1½ inches thick for the body, and two blocks 4 inches long by 2 inches wide by ½ inch thick for the wings. Make sure the grain runs lengthwise in all three pieces for strength and ease of carving.

Cut out the profile of the body and the two wings with a band saw or coping saw.

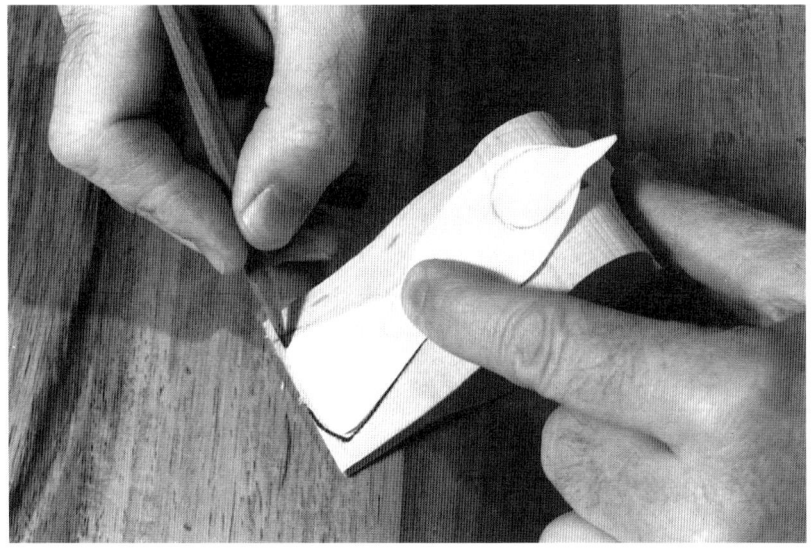

Set the wing blanks aside and trace the top view of the parula warbler on the top of the body blank. Because the back of the blank is curved, trace the tail portion of the pattern first.

Then, slide the pattern forward and trace the head.

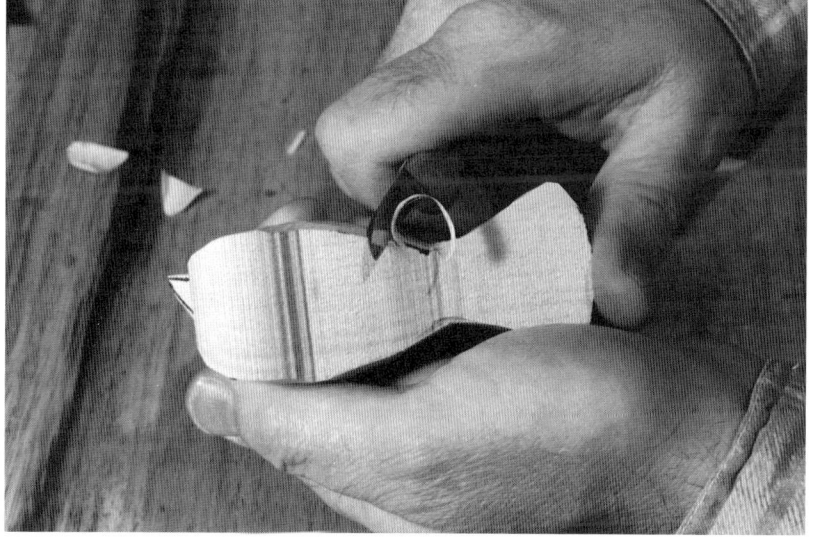

Use a carving knife to remove the excess wood outside the lines you have drawn.

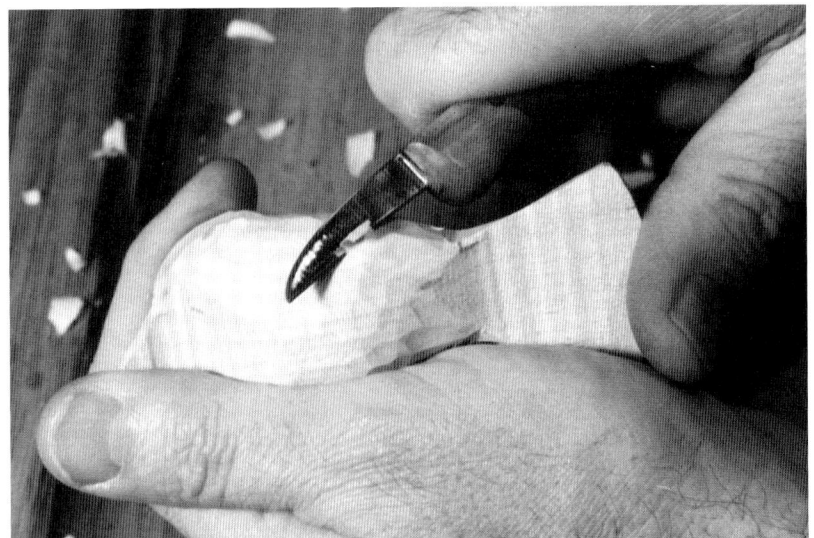

Next, round off the square corners on the body. The body is similar in shape to the first project, the blackburnian warbler.

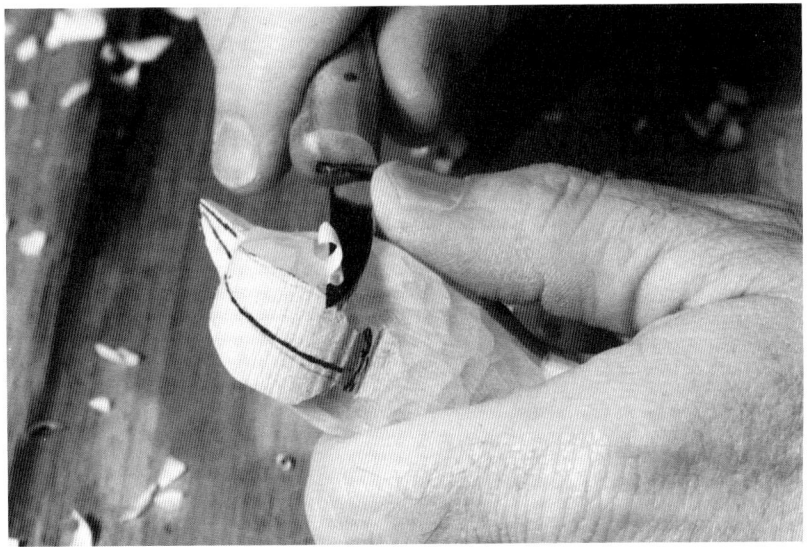

Draw a centerline on the head showing the angle at which it is turned. Then, thin the head and neck starting from the shoulders and working up toward the head to create a sleek, smooth shape.

Round the head the same way you did on the second project, the magnolia warbler.

Now, looking from the top, thin the beak so that it measures $7/32$ inch wide at the base. Be especially careful carving the beak. The parula warbler's head is turned and also tipped downward. This means that the grain runs across the beak from side to side at a 45-degree angle rather than straight from base to tip.

Remove the wood in thin, tiny chips without putting too much pressure on the beak. Be aware of the grain direction as you carve—be ready to stop and approach a cut from the opposite direction at the first sign you are carving against the grain. If you have any questions, refer to the section on carving with the grain in Getting Started.

Check the pattern for the correct shape of the warbler's beak when viewed from the side. Then adjust the shape with your carving knife. Once again, watch the wood grain carefully. In general you will be carving away from the head on the top of the beak and toward the head on the bottom of the beak.

After the beak looks right from both the top and side views, shape it the same way you did the beaks on the other two warblers. The top half is somewhat triangular, and the bottom half is rounded.

Because the beak is so fragile, I strengthened it with a coat of clear nail polish before going on to the next step. The nail polish soaks into the wood and reinforces the fibers. Nail polish is lacquer based; it will be compatible with the spray lacquer applied to the carving before painting.

If the beak does break, simply glue the pieces back on with quick-set epoxy glue and let it cure overnight.

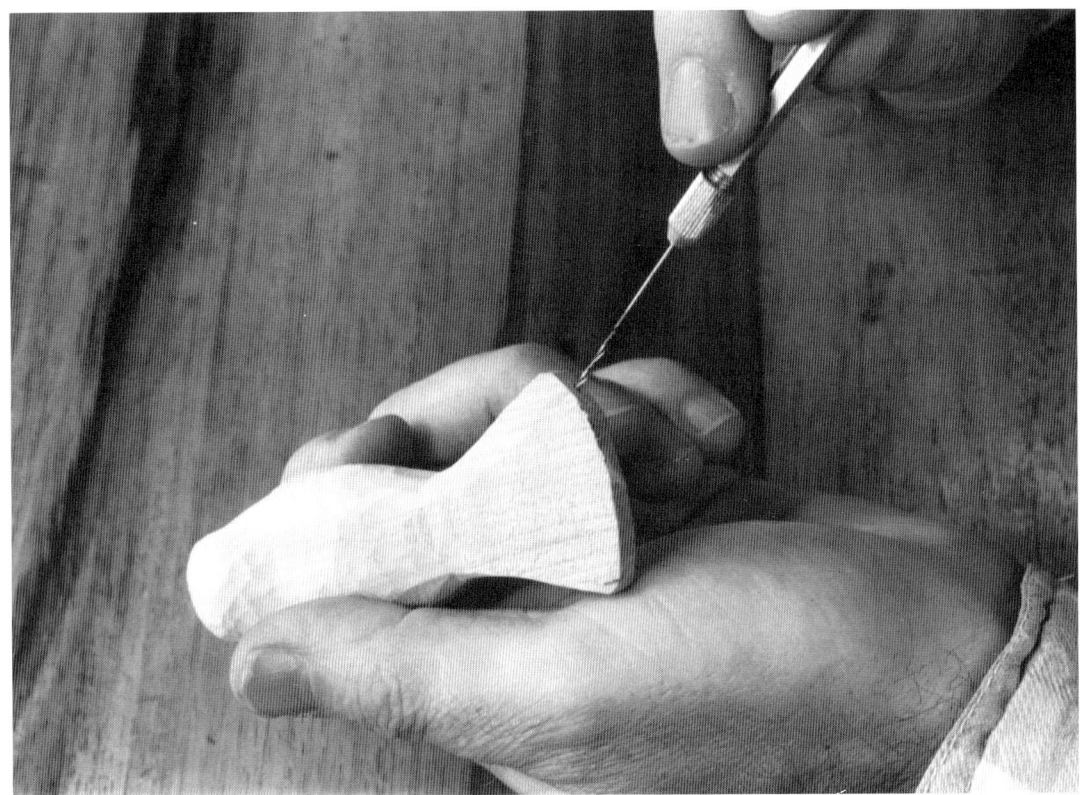

Now that the head and body are shaped, you can move to working on the tail. Begin by cutting a piece of 18-gauge copper wire about 2 inches long. Then select a drill bit that makes a hole the wire just fits into. I used a $1/32$-inch bit. Drill a practice hole in a piece of scrap wood to check the fit.

Drill a hole $1/2$ inch deep into the end of the tail. Run the hole parallel to the outer edge of the tail and as close to the middle of the wood thickness as possible. You can use an electric drill to do this, but for greater accuracy, I prefer to fasten the drill bit into a pin vise and drill the hole by hand very slowly. A pin vise, available at hobby shops and from woodworking supply catalogs, is a small metal handle with a chuck at the end large enough to hold a small drill bit.

Use an 8mm no. 5 bent gouge to hollow the underside of the tail slightly. The curved shaft of the bent gouge makes carving this area easier. Remember the position of the hole you drilled so that you don't cut into it with the gouge. In fact, you can leave the area where the hole is a little thicker than the rest of the tail. It won't show once the carving is mounted.

Next, shape the base of the undertail coverts with a 6mm no. 9 gouge.

Shape the top of the tail with the carving knife. Pay attention to the direction of the grain as you carve. At the outer edges of the tail you need to carve toward the body to avoid splitting the wood, but in the center you can carve away from the body. Remember to leave the center portion of the tail at least 1/8 inch thick for strength.

Shape the uppertail coverts with the 6mm no. 9 gouge. Use a knife to smooth the top surface of the tail, blending the shapes of the coverts and tail.

Then, thin the edges of the tail by removing paper-thin shavings from the top. Don't make the edges too thin; you can do the final, delicate shaping with sandpaper after all the carving work is completed.

Now, bevel the end of the tail to a thin edge the same way. Leave a little extra wood around the hole you drilled.

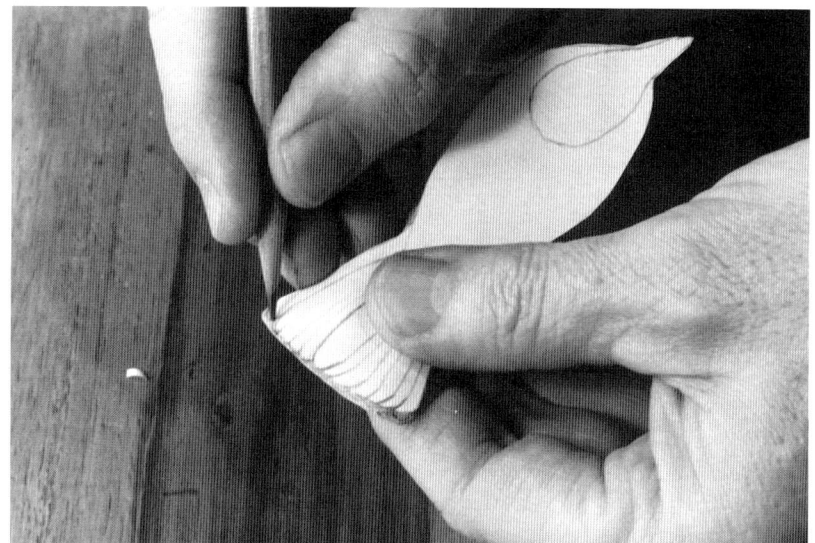

Place the top-view pattern on the tail and sketch in the feather tips. Arrange it so that the hole you drilled falls at the tip of a tail feather, not between two of them.

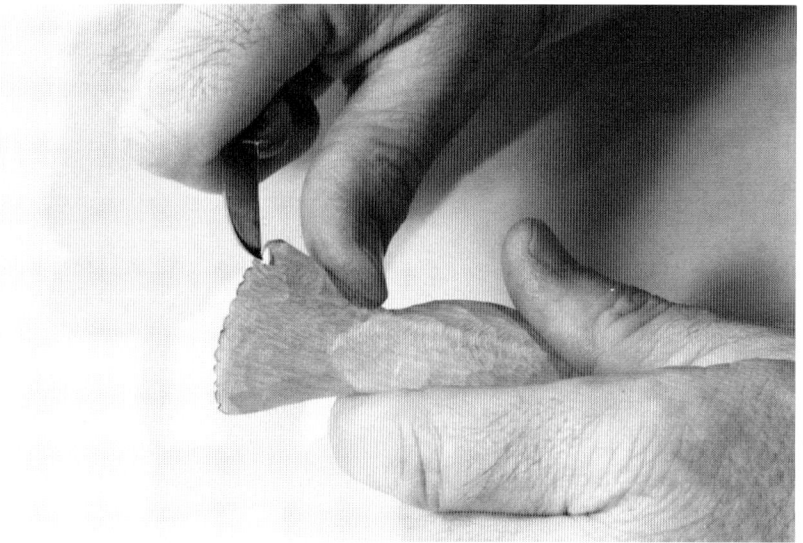

Cut tiny notches with the carving knife to serve as guides for burning-in the tail feathers.

At this point the carving of the body is done. Set it aside in a safe place where the beak won't be damaged or bumped.

Now comes the fun part, carving the wings! Don't be afraid of this step; it looks more intimidating than it really is.

Begin by drawing a line on the front, or leading, edge of the wing indicating the curve. The wing should be about ¼ inch thick at the thickest point and taper toward the top. I highly recommend sketching both wings at the same time to make sure you end up with one right wing and one left wing. It's always embarrassing to find you have carved two left wings. You may find it helpful to label the wings left, right, top, and bottom.

Begin by removing the excess wood on the top of the wing. Fasten the wing to your bench and shape it with a 12mm no. 7 gouge.

For safety reasons, *never* hold a carving on a bench with one hand and carve toward it with a gouge in your other hand. Many injuries have resulted from this incorrect technique. Always find a way of securing the wood so you can keep both hands safely on the tool. Review the section on gouge use in Getting Started if you have any questions about using carving gouges on a project like this.

My workbench and vise have a series of square holes in the surface into which special pegs called "bench dogs" can be placed to grip the wood while it is being carved. When carving an irregularly shaped blank it sometimes helps to place a small block of wood between a dog and the carving to hold it better. If you don't have a bench, you can carve the wing with a knife. It will just take a little longer.

Then turn the wing over and remove the excess wood on the bottom with a 12mm no. 7 gouge. Once again, make sure the wing is securely fastened to the bench, keep both hands on the tool, and carve away from yourself.

Next, use the same tool to hollow the underside of the wing slightly. The lower surface of the wing is concave, while the upper surface is convex. This shape is similar to the profile of an airplane wing and is what creates lift when the bird is flying.

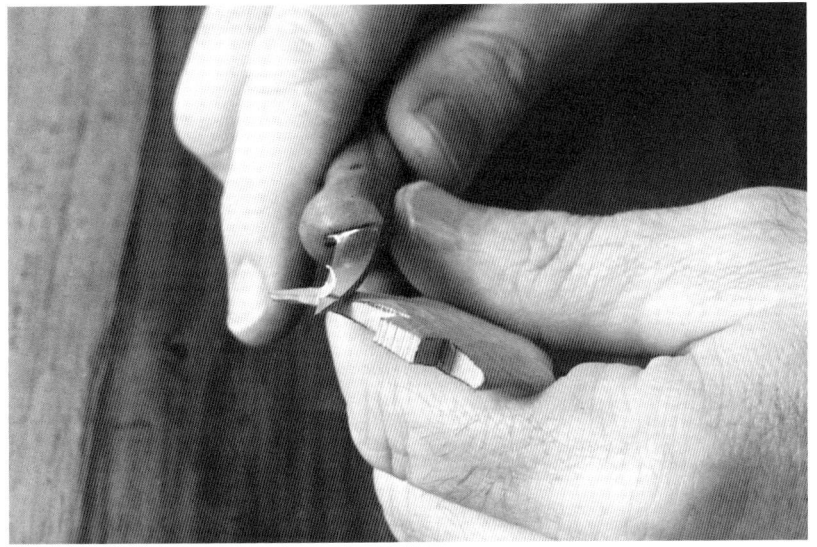

Remove the wing from the bench and use the knife to round the top surface. Then bevel the edges to make them thinner. A trick I use to make sure the wing is not getting too thin is to hold it up to a strong light and see how much light shines through. If you have any noticeably bright spots, don't remove any more wood in that area. The wing is like the tail; although the edges are thin, the center is considerably thicker, about $3/16$ inch.

The front edge of the wing is thicker than the back edge because the structure there contains bone and muscle, while the back edge is made of only the tips of the primary and secondary feathers.

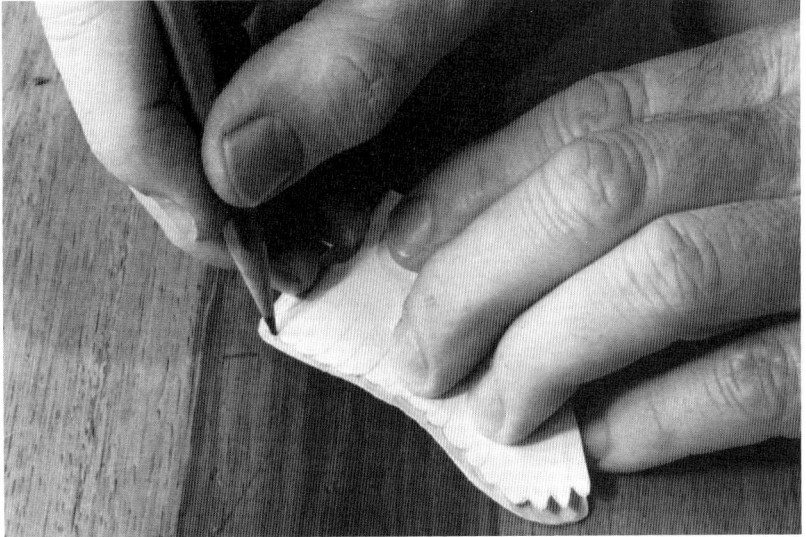

Place the wing pattern on the underside of the wing and sketch in the feather tips with a pencil.

Cut tiny notches with a carving knife to show the separation between the flight feathers. These notches will also serve as guides when you burn-in the wing feathers. If you happen to break one of the tiny feather tips off, don't worry. Just adjust the shape of the wing slightly.

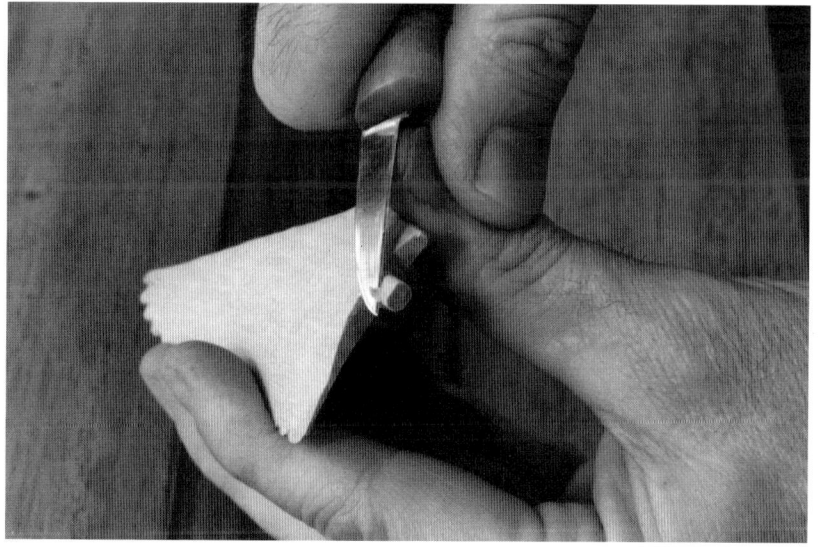

The final step in shaping the wing is to round the little tab of wood that will be inserted into the body.

After the carving is completed, I sand it very lightly with fine 280-grit garnet or aluminum oxide paper. On most of the bird I sand just enough to mellow the tool marks but not remove them completely. In the areas where the large flight and tail feathers will be burned-in, however, I sand the surface smooth so that the woodburned lines will be straight and even.

Sandpaper can also be used to make small adjustments in the shape of the feather tips on the wings and tail.

I also sand the beak very gently. Remember, it is fragile!

The technique for burning-in the feather details on the parula warbler is essentially the same as for the blackburnian and magnolia. Once again, keep a scrap of wood handy to test the temperature of the woodburning tip.

Before woodburning, sketch in lines showing the feather arrangement. This is where the notches you carved on the wing and tail tips come in handy. They help ensure that the feathers on the top and underside are aligned. Remember to overlap the feathers on the wings and tail the right way. The only feather that shows fully on the top of the tail is the center one, like the ridge line on a roof.

Use the 4-C tip on the woodburning pen on a medium heat setting. On my Detail Master this is about setting number 7, but it varies a bit on different parts of the wood. Begin by burning-in the feathers on the top of the tail. Be careful to avoid the hole you drilled. Your lines should go on either side of it.

Then, turn the carving over and burn-in the underside of the tail.

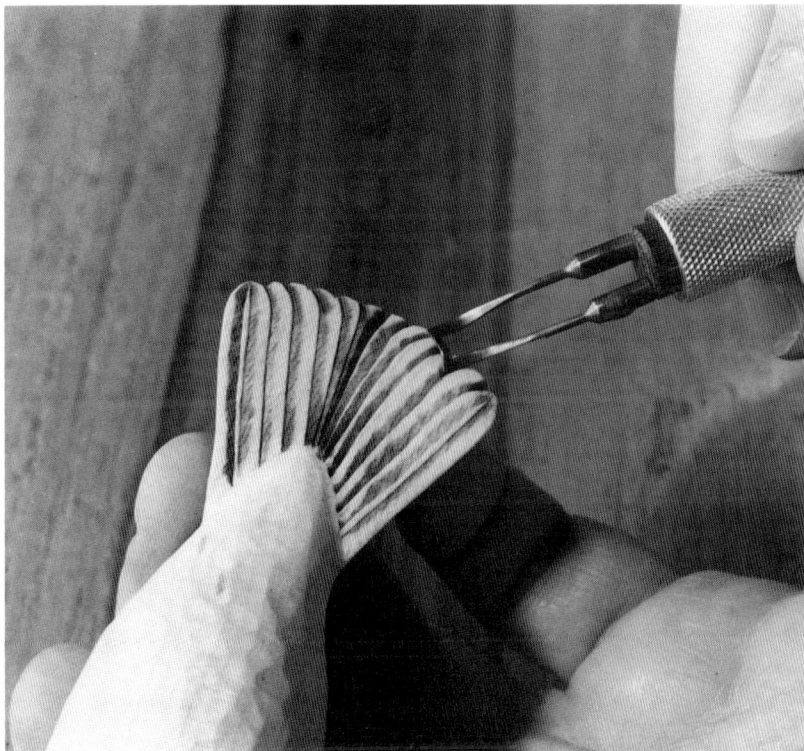

Now, use the woodburning pen to shape the separation between the tail feathers at the tip of the tail.

Burn-in the feathers on the underside of the wing.

Next, burn-in the feathers on the top of the wing. Burn-in the tips of the wing feathers the same way you did the tip of the tail.

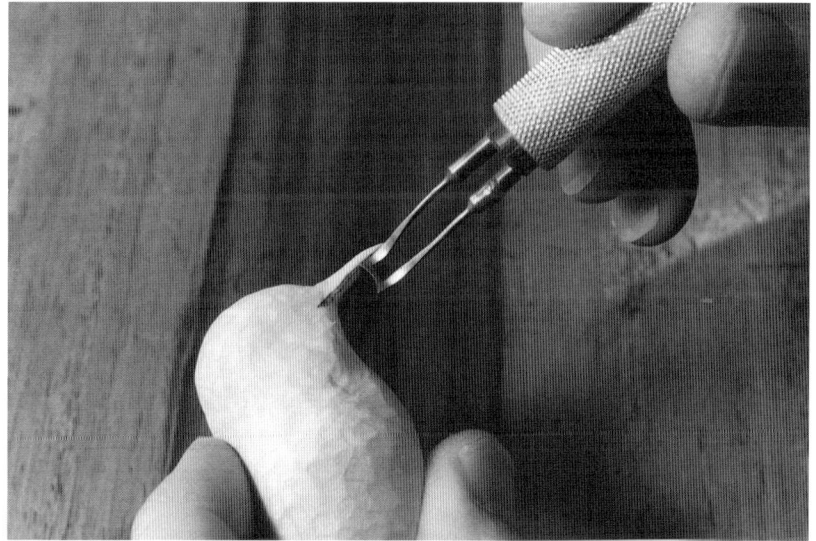

Burn-in the lines showing the separation between the upper and lower mandibles.

Then, create nostrils with the tip of the woodburning pen.

Mark the position of the legs with a pencil, then make a small starter hole with a scratch awl. Carefully screw a holding stick into one of the leg holes.

Seal the body and wings with a light coat of spray lacquer, such as Deft Semi-Gloss Clear Wood Finish. Let the lacquer dry thoroughly, following the manufacturer's recommendations.

While the lacquer is drying, paint the backs of a pair of 5mm clear glass eyes brown with burnt umber acrylic paint. Let the paint dry.

Then insert the eyes. This is a small change from the two earlier projects, in which the eyes were inserted after the carving was undercoated with gesso; it is easier to hold the bird and carve eye holes before the outstretched wings are added. The flying parula warbler will be undercoated after the wings and body are assembled.

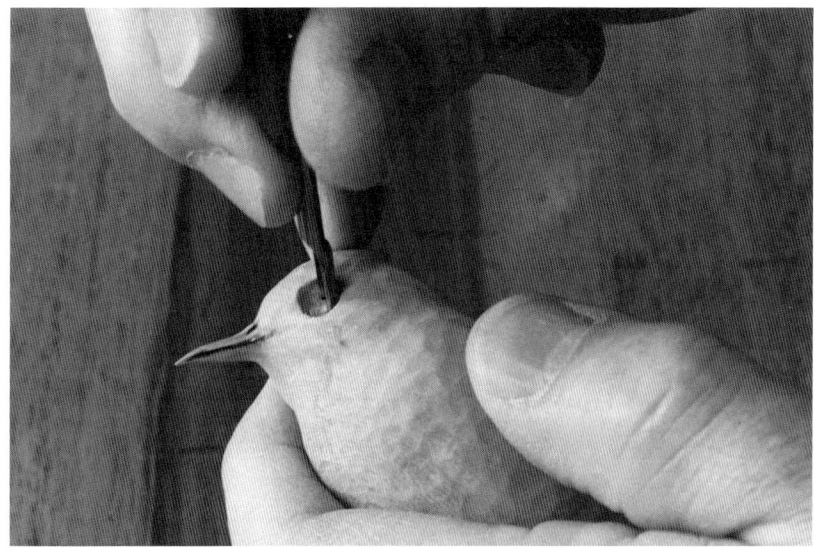

Sketch in the position of the eyes, checking that they look level from both the top and the front. Carve a hole for the eyes with a tiny 4mm no. 9 gouge.

Mix some epoxy putty, making sure the two components of the putty are mixed completely so it will harden properly. Place a small ball of putty in each eye socket and carefully press the glass eyes down into it.

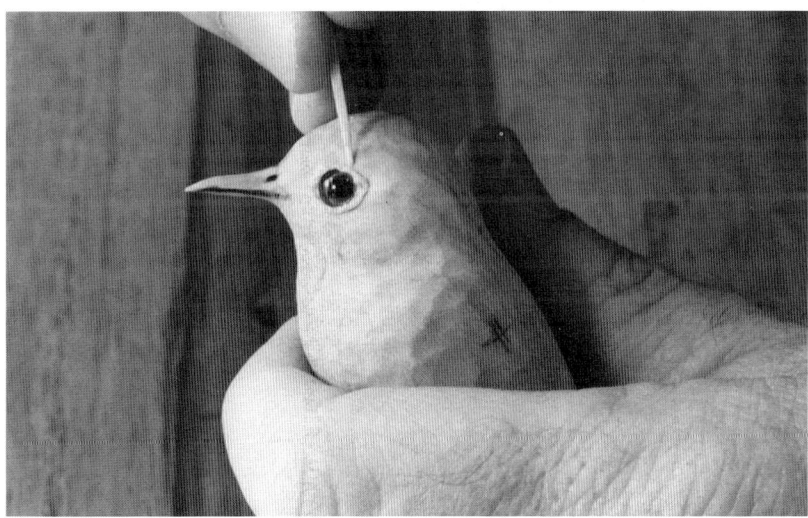

A little putty will ooze out around the eye as you press it in. Use this excess putty to form an eyelid. Shape the eyelid with the flat end of a toothpick, then use the pointed end to detail the skin texture of the eyelid. Let the putty harden before going on to the next step.

Parula Warbler • 105

Now you are ready to put the wings on the parula warbler. Start by marking the position of the holes on the sides of the body. Use the pattern as a rough guide for placement, adjusting the position a little if necessary to suit the shape of your particular bird. No two are ever exactly alike.

I use a small gouge, such as a 3mm or 4mm no. 9, to carve the wing holes into the bird's body. I prefer the gouge to a drill because a drill is likely to rip and splinter the wood. Carve the hole the same way you carved the eye holes, aiming for vertical sides and a relatively flat bottom.

Test-fit the peg into the hole as you go. You can also shape the peg itself for a smoother fit. The fit does not have to be perfect, but enough of the peg has to be in contact with the sides of the hole to form a good glue joint.

You will probably have to adjust the shape of the wing so that it fits well against the body. Make sure your knife is razor sharp, as you are cutting across the grain. A dull knife will crush and tear the wood. Remove the wood in paper-thin shavings and check the fit frequently; you don't want to take too much off.

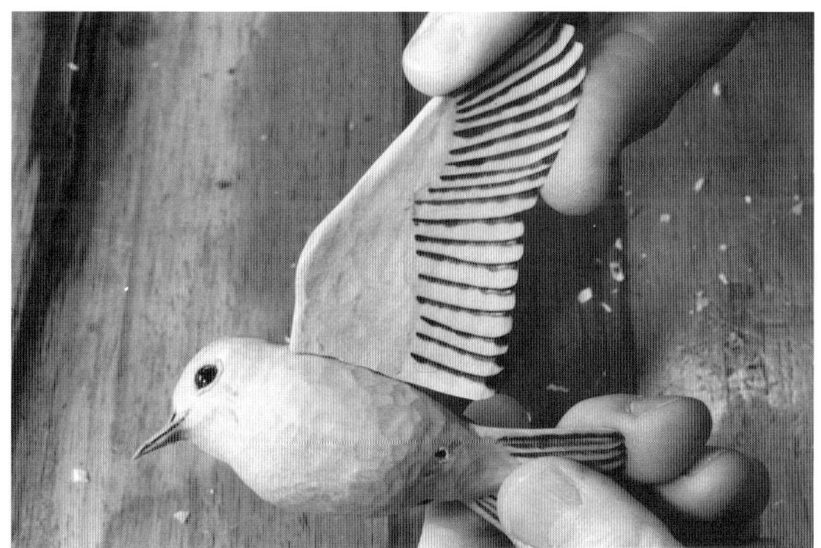

Get the fit as close as you can, but don't worry about making it perfect. Any small gaps will be smoothed over later with epoxy putty.

When both wings are adjusted the way you like them, glue them in place with quick-set epoxy glue. Glue the wings in one at a time and simply hold them in place until the glue sets.

Parula Warbler • **107**

After the glue has set, use epoxy putty to smooth the wing joints and blend the wing and body shapes together. Mix the two components of the putty and then make a "worm" of putty about ⅛ inch in diameter and long enough to wrap around the entire base of the wing.

To smooth the putty, dip your finger in water and flatten the putty, working it well into the joint. Feather the edges into the body, making the transition between the putty and the wood as smooth as possible. When the putty hardens, it will also strengthen the wing joint, making your warbler much more durable.

Undercoat the parula warbler with white gesso after the putty has hardened. Apply a thin, even coat with a soft, medium-size paintbrush, such as a no. 4 flat synthetic sable. Make your brush strokes in the direction that the feather barbs lie.

PAINTING

For detailed instructions on painting the parula warbler, please refer to the chapter on painting techniques.

MOUNTING

There are two options for mounting the flying parula warbler. You can attach feet to the bird the same way you did with the blackburnian and magnolia and mount it by the feet as though it were just landing, but I prefer a tail mount to give the illusion of free flight. For this mounting the base is prepared the same way as for the previous two projects, but the branch you attach to it may be shaped differently. Avoid a branch that goes straight up and down. A curved branch or one mounted at a diagonal will give your carving a greater sense of life and movement. The branch I chose for the parula warbler is 8 inches long, with the warbler mounted about halfway up.

Look carefully at the proportions of your base and branch before you glue them together. A small, 4-inch-diameter base works well with the slender branch I used, but if you use a larger branch, you might want a 5- or 6-inch-diameter base for better proportions and balance.

If you mount the parula warbler in free flight, you will have to modify the pewter feet for a realistic flight position. To do this, use a pair of wire cutters to snip off the central mounting post below the feet.

Because the feet don't need to support the weight of the bird, you don't have to insert them very far into the body. So, next trim off most of the post at the top of the leg and use a small metal file to narrow the knee joint. This means you can drill smaller holes in the body for a neater mounting job.

Then carefully bend the toes into a loosely closed position. I find it helps to file small notches on the underside of the toes where they would naturally bend. This reduces the stress on the toes when you bend them, and lessens the danger of breaking.

Because the feet have been trimmed, they can be a little tricky to hold while you paint. The best system I have found is to grip them in locking hemostats, also known as kelly clamps. These are inexpensive medical clamps available from medical supply stores, hobby shops, and art supply catalogs. I find them handy because they come to a fine point. Also, they have a locking device in the handle so they can grip a small object and hold it securely. In a pinch, small needle-nose pliers are an acceptable substitute.

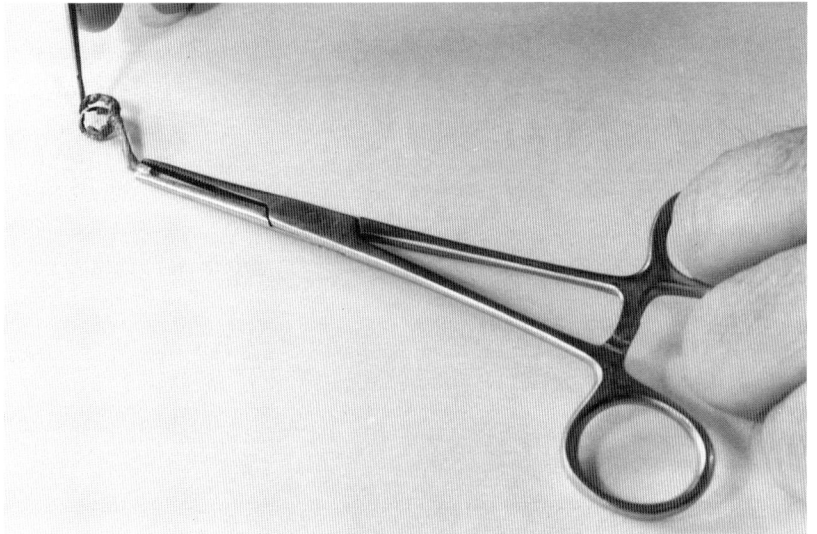

A parula warbler's feet are a brownish orange. Mix a bright orange acrylic, such as Indo Orange Red, with yellow ochre light to mute it. Then, darken it with a touch of burnt umber. Paint the whole foot, then darken the claws with a thin wash of burnt umber.

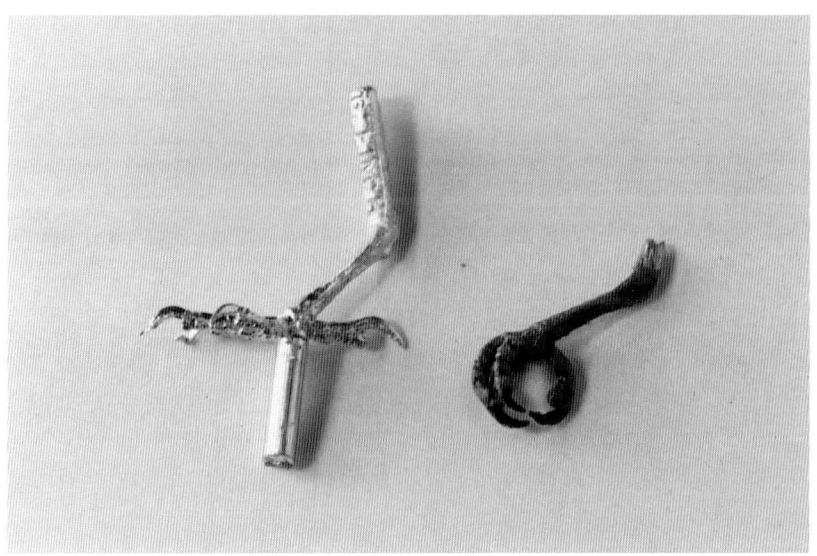

This is how the original foot looked, and how the finished foot looks.

Glue the feet in with quick-set epoxy. After the glue has set, you can touch up around the base of the legs with a little acrylic paint.

Now, glue a length of 18-gauge copper wire about 2 inches long into the hole in the tail. For best results, sand the wire lightly with fine sandpaper before you glue it in. This cleans and roughs up the surface for a better glue bond.

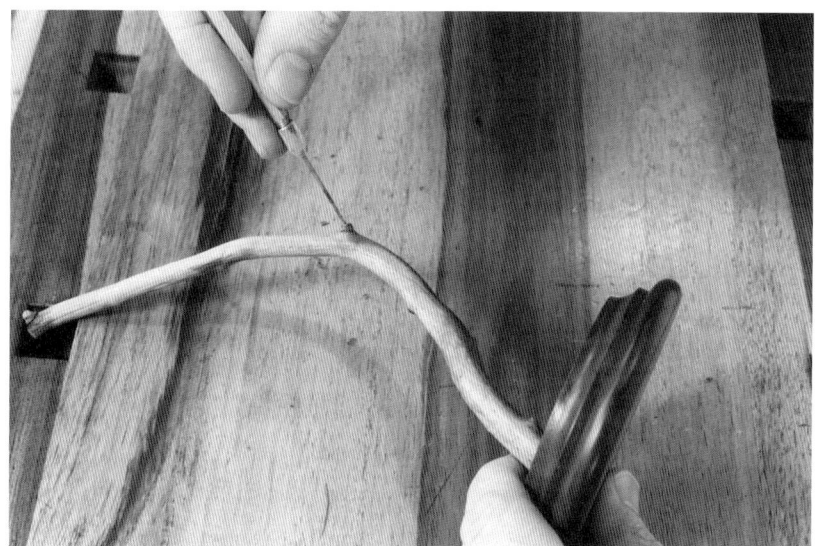

Use a tiny drill bit in the pin vise to drill a hole into the branch, the same way you drilled a hole in the tail earlier. I used a 1/32-inch bit.

The hole in the branch should be between 1/4 and 1/2 inch deep; it does not have to be too deep because the bird is very light and does not need heavy-duty support. It is important not to drill all the way through the branch, so work slowly and carefully.

Test-fit the wire in the hole, and then trim it off short enough that the bird's tail rests against the branch. Then, glue the warbler to the base with quick-set epoxy glue. Put glue both on the wire and inside the hole in the base (a needle is handy for this). Carefully wipe off any excess glue, then hold the bird in place until the glue sets.

Although a free-flying mounting takes a little more time, it is certainly the most striking and dramatic method of displaying any bird, and it is well worth the effort.

Painting Warblers

Some woodcarvers get the impression that painting is some dark mystery accessible only to the artistically talented, but it really is a skill you can learn, just like carving. All it takes is a little practice and experience, and you will be able to get the results you want and even have fun painting your carvings.

There are many different ways to paint songbirds. The painting method that I have developed has its roots in the nineteenth-century French Impressionist style. These artists were searching for new ways of using paint to create a fresh, spontaneous effect that conveyed a feeling of life and personality. The paint was applied to create the *appearance* of fine details in the mind of the viewer. These methods can be modified to work quite well with songbirds by recreating the feeling of soft feathers, personality, and essential details without sacrificing technical accuracy.

PAINTING TECHNIQUES

Before you begin painting your carvings, read this section on painting carefully. It will help you become familiar with the methods I use for painting songbirds and the terms used to describe the various techniques. Then, practice these techniques on a smooth, nonabsorbent surface until you feel confident handling the paints and brushes.

A small pane of glass about 6 or 8 inches square makes a good surface to practice on. Tape the edges with masking tape so that they don't cut you and just play around with different methods of blending colors. The nice thing about a glass surface is that you can clean the paint off and use it again and again. This pane of glass also makes an excellent palette for mixing your paints when you actually start painting a carving.

The basic materials you need for painting in this style are alkyd paints, acrylic paints, and a selection of brushes.

Alkyd paints are a fairly new development in the art world. They have the same pigments as oil paints, and they thin with paint thinner or turpentine, as oil paints do. More important, they blend just like oil paints for subtle painting techniques. They differ from oil paints by having a base of alkyd resin rather than linseed oil. This means they have all the advantages of oil paint but dry in a day or two instead of weeks. Winsor & Newton makes a complete line of alkyds called Griffin Alkyd Colours, available at large art supply stores and through mail order catalogs.

The other type of paint I use is acrylic, a plastic emulsion in a water base. Acrylic paints can be thinned with water and brushed on to make very fine lines, and they dry in a matter of minutes. I like them for fine finishing details and shading after the alkyd base coat has dried. Acrylic paints are available everywhere art supplies are sold.

Brushes are one of the most important components of any painting system. I recommend buying the best brushes you can find and caring for them meticulously. Never let paint dry on brushes, especially acrylic paint, as it ruins them. Clean your brushes frequently as you work, and wash them all thoroughly when you are finished painting. Don't leave them standing on their tips in solvent or water. This damages the bristles and distorts the shape of the brush. A well-cared-for paintbrush will last for years.

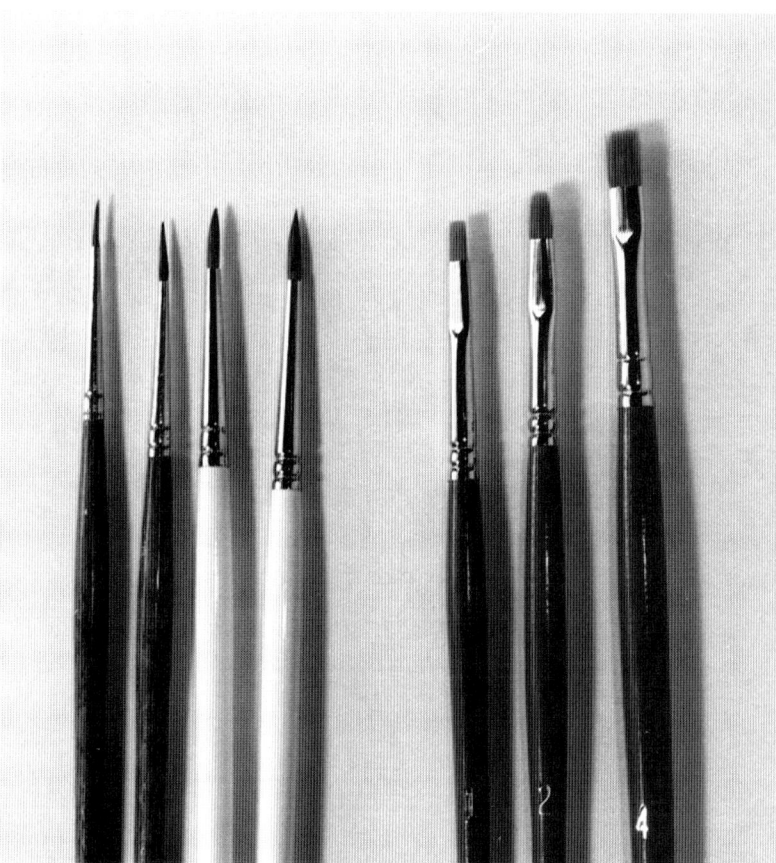

I recommend three basic types of brushes for songbird painting: small, soft, pointed brushes; flat brushes; and blending brushes.

In brush sizing, lower numbers are smaller. This means that a no. 00 is smaller than a no. 0. Select a range of small, soft, pointed brushes sized from no. 000 to no. 1. For this type of brush natural red sable bristles are best, as they come to a fine point and hold it well for very delicate detail work. For sizes larger than no. 1, a good-quality synthetic sable is fine.

Choose some flat brushes with soft, fine, synthetic sable bristles in a range of sizes from no. 0 to no. 4 or no. 6. These brushes are the workhorses of songbird painting, used to lay down the basic color areas on the carvings.

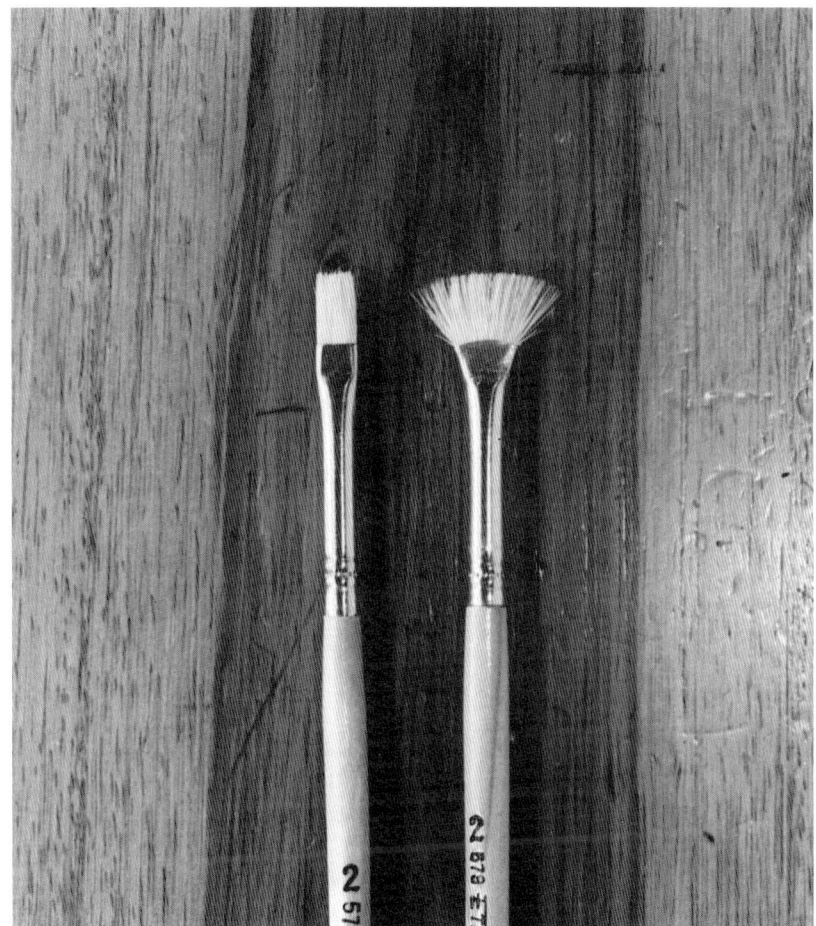

For fine, feathery details, a blending brush with fanned-out bristles is essential. Most fan blenders on the market, however, are much too large for delicate songbird painting. I make my own. I start with inexpensive flat, china bristle brushes in a range of sizes from no. 0 to no. 4. Then I lay them down flat on a hard metal surface and hit the metal ferrule around the base of the bristles gently with a hammer until the ferrule flattens and the bristles fan out. This makes a great little blending brush, smaller and more precise than anything you can buy.

These china bristle blenders are good for blending paints right on the birds to create subtle feathery effects. The stiff bristles can also cut through the paint to give it a fine feather texture, and they are perfect for dry brushing techniques with acrylic paint.

The first technique to try with alkyd paint is called *hard-edge blending*. This is used where two colors meet with a sharply defined edge, like the black eye patch on the magnolia warbler. Practice by painting a stripe of white next to a darker color.

Next, take a china bristle blending brush and gently and slowly drag a bit of dark paint into the white. Wipe the paint off your brush with a dry, lint-free cloth and repeat the motion again. Repeat this until you have blended the entire length of the stripe.

The next technique is called *soft-edge blending*. This is used where one color of feathers is gradually toned into another color, such as the green and blue colors on the back of the parula warbler.

Practice by using the alkyd paints and two stripes of different colors, such as white and burnt umber. Take a clean synthetic sable brush and, using a gentle up-and-down motion, blend the two colors into each other. Notice that each up-and-down motion of the brush picks up a little color from one area and transfers it to the next. This type of blending is called *stippling*.

When you have "softened" the edge between the two colors, use a bristle blending brush and gently and slowly drag paint from one color into the other, just as in the first technique. This produces a feathery appearance of one color gradually shading into the other.

Experiment with these techniques until you have a feeling for what effects you can create with alkyd paints and your brushes.

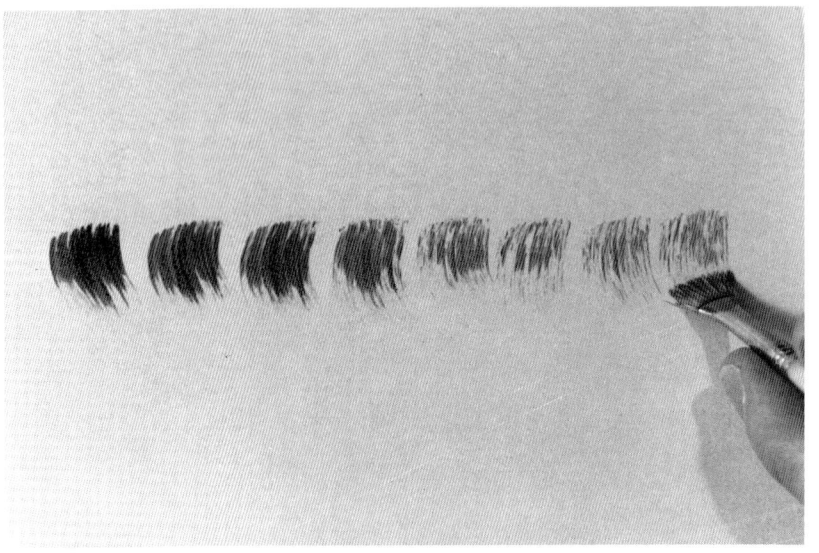

Likewise, the water-based acrylic paints are well suited for use with the dry-brushing technique. This is a good way to add subtle feather shading on your carving after the alkyd base coat has dried. Practice by making a thin mixture of burnt umber acrylic and water in a small plate or saucer. Dip the end of a bristle blending brush into the mixture and make a series of brush strokes on a piece of smooth paper. You will notice that as the paint is drawn off the brush, each stroke deposits less paint and the lines become more feathery. When the brush is nearly dry, you will notice that the bristles leave fine lines of paint instead of a dark glob. This is the effect you want. With a little practice you can create a variety of shading and texturing strokes on your carving.

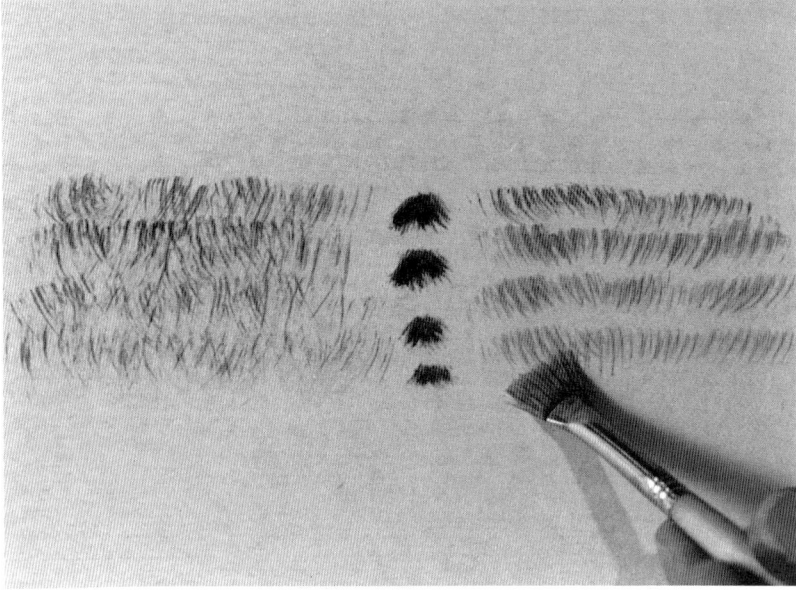

Blackburnian Warbler

Before you begin painting a carving, think through your strategy for the best results. The blackburnian warbler is a bird with a base color of brilliant orange and an overlying black color with sharply defined edges.

For this reason I decided to approach the painting in three stages. First, paint and blend the foundation coat of orange and white, and let it dry. Then apply black paint for the back, the face pattern, and the chest spots. Finally, when the black paint is dry, add the fine details, such as the white wing bars and feather shading.

Make an intense orange by mixing some cadmium red medium with cadmium yellow medium alkyd paint. Begin by painting the underparts of the bird with titanium white from the undertail coverts to the midchest with a medium-size brush, such as a no. 2 flat synthetic sable.

Then paint a 3/8-inch-wide band of cadmium yellow medium above the white. Don't worry about making this too precise; the colors will all be blended together smoothly. Then, paint the face and top of the head orange. Any paint that gets on the eyes can be cleaned off easily later. When the paint is dry, simply scrape it off gently with the point of a pocketknife. (Don't use your carving knife, or you will dull the blade.)

Where two colors meet, use stippling to soften the line of demarcation between the colors. Stipple between the white and yellow first, and then between the yellow and orange.

Then, to create a gradual transition from one color to the next, use a small blending brush. Mine is made from a no. 3 china bristle brush. Begin at the top of the head and make light feathery strokes, dragging the orange paint into the yellow and then the yellow into the white. Wipe your brush clean between every few strokes. Let the white and orange foundation dry for a day or two until it is dry to the touch.

After the white and orange paint is dry, you can very lightly pencil in some guidelines for the black paint. This step is optional, and I usually just "wing it."

Mix a warm black by adding a touch of burnt umber to ivory black alkyd paint. If necessary, thin the paint with a drop of turpentine or paint thinner to a smooth brushing consistency.

Use a no. 4 flat synthetic sable brush to apply the paint to the bird's back. Start at the tail and work forward toward the head. Then, use a smaller brush, such as a no. 0 round sable, to paint the markings on the face and the spots on the breast. Make the markings on the face and the spots slightly smaller and thinner than you want them to appear on the finished warbler. They will widen slightly when you blend them.

Before the paint dries, use a small blender made from a no. 1 china bristle to very gently stroke the black paint over the orange where the two colors meet. Keep your blender clean and dry by wiping it between strokes on a clean, lint-free cloth. Use a very light touch to gently drag a wisp of black paint over the orange, leaving a soft feathery edge.

Then, use the same blender to texture the black paint on the rest of the body by making short strokes with the blender in the direction the feathers grow.

Painting Warblers • 123

Use the same techniques for the underside of the tail. Mix a medium gray by adding titanium white to the black you made earlier. First, apply the paint to the undertail in a thin, even coat. Then, very lightly blend the gray over the white of the undertail coverts to create a soft, feathered edge. Use the blender to texture the undertail, making short brush strokes in the direction the barbs on the tail feathers grow.

After the black paint is thoroughly dry, you can add the finishing details. As discussed earlier, I prefer to use water-based acrylic paint for the final details, as it dries quickly and can be thinned with water to make very subtle effects. If the acrylic paint shows a tendency to "bead up" on the carving, simply add a small drop of dish detergent or acrylic wetting agent (sold at art supply stores) to the paint mixture. This will release the surface tension of the water and allow you to apply the paint in a consistent, thin film.

To begin, use the no. 1 china bristle blender you made to highlight the edges of the tail and wing feathers. The color is titanium white with just a touch of ultramarine blue to suggest the bluish daylight of the bird's natural outdoor habitat. Straight white would appear chalky. Because acrylics tend to darken slightly when they dry, I always mix them just a bit lighter than I want the finished color to appear.

Use the dry-brush technique to very lightly drag a little color over the edges of the tail and wing feathers. Move the brush diagonally from the edge of the feather toward the central shaft in the same direction the barbs lie on a real feather.

This technique reproduces the subtle edging of lighter color on the feathers. It also creates highlights along the outer edges of the feathers to enhance the illusion of depth and separation.

The beauty of acrylic paint is that if you don't like what you've done, you can change it. The paint will wipe off easily with a damp tissue right after you've put it on. This won't affect the alkyd base coat if you have allowed it to dry thoroughly.

The edging will dry very quickly, so you can move on to the next step, the white wing bars on the coverts and the white stripes on the mantle. Use the dry-brushing technique with the no. 1 china bristle blender to apply the paint. I use straight titanium white acrylic for this step. Do some practice strokes on a small pad of paper to make sure you have the right amount of paint on your brush. If the paint seems too thick, you can add a drop or two of water for a smooth brushing consistency.

For the next step you will need a tiny, pointed sable brush, such as a no. 0 or no. 000. Use ivory black acrylic for the final painted details. Thin the paint with water and add a tiny drop of dish detergent or wetting agent if necessary to prevent beading. Then, very carefully paint the lower wing edges next to the breast with the acrylic black. Also touch up under the wing tips if necessary.

Use the same brush to redefine the woodburned lines showing the flight and tail feathers if they were painted over when you did the white edging or wing bars. Just outline the feathers very carefully with black.

Also continue the black eye stripe through the eyelid by painting it in with the tiny pointed brush.

When you undercoated the blackburnian warbler with gesso, you left the beak unpainted. I like to paint the beak with a thin coat of semitransparent alkyd paint, allowing some of the natural wood color to show through. I feel this best recreates the translucent horn a bird's beak is composed of. I use alkyd paint on the beak because it dries more slowly than acrylic, giving you more time to achieve the desired effect.

Use burnt umber darkened with a little black to create a deep, warm gray. Apply it to the beak with a medium-size flat brush, such as a no. 2 synthetic sable. Use a small, pointed no. 1 sable brush to paint the very base of the beak so that you don't brush any of the dark beak color onto the face. Apply a thin, even coat of paint, then clean and dry the brush. To create the translucent look, stroke the beak gently from the base toward the tip until the color lightens to the shade you want. If you remove too much paint, it is easy to add a little more and start over.

Mounting the finished carving is covered in the blackburnian warbler chapter.

Magnolia Warbler

Before you begin painting the magnolia warbler, you may find it helpful to pencil some very light guidelines on the carving. Be sure to keep them faint so that they don't show through the paint on the finished carving.

These days I usually paint without guidelines. From years of observation I have learned that most warblers' color patterns don't exactly match the precise drawings shown in guidebooks. There is a lot of variation among individual birds, and their feathers are often slightly mussed. I have discovered that applying the paint somewhat freely creates a more natural, lifelike effect.

I used a technique called wet on wet, or alla prima, to paint this warbler. Rather than painting on some colors, letting them dry, and then adding others, I painted the entire carving at one time.

The magnolia warbler's plumage is more muted than the blackburnian's, with less contrast between the colors. The wet-on-wet technique captures the soft shading perfectly. Alkyd paints are particularly well suited to this style because they handle just like oil paints and blend beautifully. They also dry more quickly. The final details will be done with acrylic paint.

Make a pale blue-gray for the back of the bird by mixing ultramarine blue, burnt umber, and titanium white. Then use a medium-size, flat brush, such as a no. 4, to apply the paint. I like to start at the tail and work forward for both painting and blending.

Add some more titanium white to the color to lighten it, and paint the underside of the tail and wings.

While the paint is still soft and wet, use a blending brush made from a no. 1 flat, china bristle brush to texture it. The object is to make brush strokes in the same direction that the feathers lie on a living bird. On the large feathers of the wings and tail, make smooth, diagonal strokes to indicate the barbs on the feathers. On the body use short, light strokes for the soft, fine body feathers. When the paint dries, it will have a very fine feather texture.

Paint the white spot above the eye and the white spots on the top and bottom of the tail with titanium white using a no. 2 flat brush.

Now, with the small blender, brush the white over the blue the same way you did on the blackburnian warbler to create a soft "feather edge" between two colors. Be sure to wipe your brush clean between each stroke to avoid contamination.

Next, add a touch of burnt umber to ivory black. The burnt umber will warm the color and also speed the drying time. Paint the black eye patch with a small brush. Don't apply black paint to the lower third of the eyelid; it will be painted white when you detail the carving.

Then, blend the black paint with the no. 1 china bristle blender.

Mix a soft yellow with cadmium yellow light and titanium white. Use a small, flat, no. 2 brush to paint the rump and the underside of the magnolia warbler yellow. I like to brush a little more titanium white right into the yellow paint of the lower abdomen and undertail coverts. When you texture the feathers, the white and yellow will blend together for a subtle, shaded effect.

Then blend the yellow over the blue to create a feather edge between the two colors. Work carefully on this step. Clean your brush frequently between strokes, and only make one pass with the brush in each area. Remember, you are working wet on wet. If you overwork the colors with repeated brush strokes, the blue and yellow will mix and create green. After blending, texture the feathers with the blending brush the same way you did the blue on the back.

The final step with the alkyd paint is to blend the black eye patch into the yellow throat. Don't try to blend the yellow up into the black. It usually works best to work from a dark color into a lighter one. Also, blending the black into the yellow follows the way the feathers naturally grow. Keep your brush clean and don't overwork the paint. Black and yellow mix to make a sort of olive drab. This can be handy to know, but it's not the effect you want on your magnolia warbler.

Let the alkyd paint dry thoroughly. It usually takes only a day or two.

I prefer acrylic paint for the finishing details. If the water-based acrylic paint beads up on the alkyd base coat, just add a tiny drop of dish detergent or acrylic wetting agent to your paint mixture to break the surface tension of the water.

The first step is to add the very subtle, light edging on the wing and tail feathers. This step also highlights the feather details you created with the woodburning pen.

Use titanium white acrylic thinned with a little water. If you like, you can add just a touch of ultramarine blue to the white to suggest the bluish cast of natural daylight. Dry brush the paint on the wings with the no. 1 china bristle blender the same way you did for the blackburnian warbler. Keep a small pad of paper handy to test your brush on before you paint the bird. The brush should be dry enough to leave faint feathery brush strokes, not wet blobs.

Next, use titanium white to paint the distinctive white patch on the wing with the no. 1 blender. If necessary, thin the paint with water to a smooth brushing consistency. Make sure the brush strokes go in the same direction as the feather barbs. The white on the wing is one of the field marks for the magnolia warbler.

134 • Painting Warblers

Now, make a slate blue transparent wash by mixing burnt umber with ultramarine blue. Add water to create a thin, watery stain. Use a tiny, pointed no. 0 or no. 000 sable brush to paint the wash in the woodburned lines between the feathers of the wings and tail. This creates a shadow detail that enhances the separation between the feathers and makes the bird look more alive. I also use this color to paint center shafts on those feathers where they are visible.

Lighten the wash by thinning it with a little more water, and accent the feathers on the undersides of the wings and tail.

If you like, you can use the same color to add some breaks on the wing and tail feathers. Start at the bottom edge of the feather and make a short stroke upward on a diagonal following the direction of the feather barbs. This break recreates the look of a feather whose barbs have separated slightly. It adds a subtle hint of realism to the carving. The secret is to add only a few feather breaks, making sure they are randomly placed, not arranged in a regular pattern.

Paint the beak brownish black with a mixture of ivory black and burnt umber alkyd paint the same way you painted the beak on the blackburnian warbler. Apply a thin, even coat of paint. Then, clean and dry the brush and stroke the beak from base to tip to remove a little of the paint and create the translucent look of a live bird's beak.

Paint the spots on the chest and rump with ivory black acrylic paint mixed with a bit of burnt umber to warm the tone. Add a little water if necessary for a soft brushing consistency. Then paint the spots with a small pointed brush, such as a no. 2 round sable. I use a dry-brush technique and apply the paint with short, light strokes so the spots look soft and feathery.

The magnolia warbler has a partial white eye ring. The top part usually blends right in with the white eyebrow over the eye, and the bottom part circles around the bottom third of the eye. Use titanium white acrylic and paint the eye ring in with a tiny, pointed no. 0 sable brush.

If you need to, you can also touch up the black portion of the eyelid using the same small pointed brush.

I like to break up the blue-gray of the back by dry brushing on a little feather texture with the small no. 1 china bristle blender.

Make a transparent wash of acrylic paint using the same colors you used to shade the wing and tail feathers: burnt umber and ultramarine blue. If you need to lighten the color, do so by adding more water, thinning the wash. Never add white.

Dip your brush in the wash, then take a few strokes on a pad of white paper to remove the excess paint. Then, brush a little color on the carving, using a very light touch so that only the very tips of the bristles touch the carving.

Parula Warbler

I painted the parula warbler wet on wet with alkyd paints in much the same way I painted the magnolia warbler. The primaries and most of the tail feathers are a dark brownish blue made by mixing burnt umber with cerulean blue and a touch of ultramarine blue to intensify the color. Add just a little titanium white to lighten the color. Use a medium-size no. 3 or no. 4 flat synthetic sable brush.

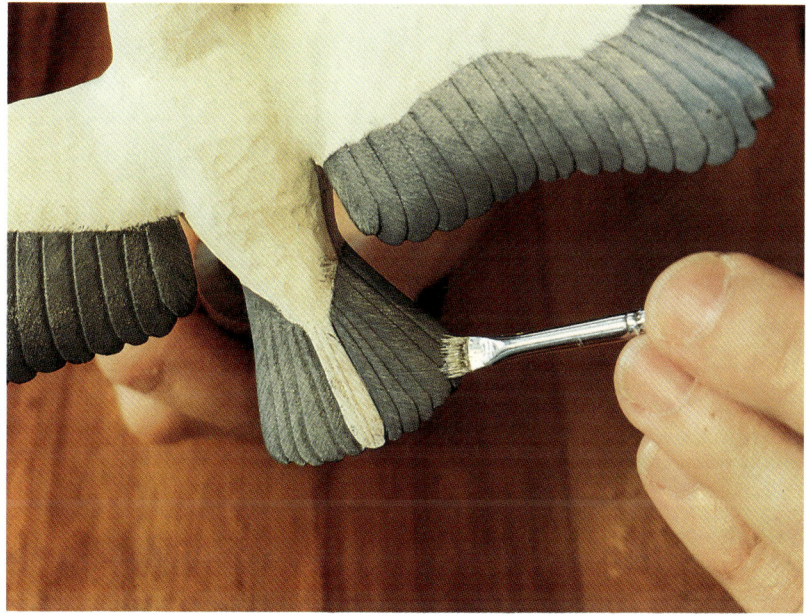

Texture the paint with the no. 1 china bristle blender in the direction the feather barbs go.

Add a little more titanium white to the color and paint the undersides of the wing and tail feathers. While the paint is still very soft and wet, texture it the same way you did the feathers on the top of the bird.

Next, mix a soft blue-gray for the head and back. This is a lighter color with less brown in it than the color used for the flight feathers. Mix cerulean blue with a touch of burnt umber to gray it. Add titanium white to lighten it to the desired shade. Paint the head, back, upperwing coverts, and uppertail coverts blue with a flat no. 2 or no. 4 brush.

One of the distinguishing marks of the parula warbler is a small patch of greenish feathers on the shoulder, or mantle. No other blue-gray bird has this coloration. An ornithologist friend described it as looking like watered silk. To make this color, paint a little yellow ochre right over the blue in the mantle area. Stipple the colors to blend them together. You are actually blending the paints right on the bird, one of the benefits of the wet-on-wet technique.

Next, use the no. 1 china bristle blender to blend the color on the upperwing coverts over the edge of the flight feathers on the wing. Do the same thing to blend the color on the rump and uppertail coverts over the darker tail feathers.

Then, use the same brush to feather the mantle color into the back. Also use the blender to texture the feathers on the back, making your brush strokes in the direction the feathers lie.

Take the basic blue-gray you mixed for the back and add some titanium white to lighten it. Paint this color on the underwing coverts with a medium-size flat brush. Blend the color over the darker flight feathers with the no. 1 bristle blender.

The next step is to paint the underparts. Mix titanium white with a tiny bit of burnt umber to warm it slightly and speed the drying time. Paint the underside of the bird, starting with the undertail coverts and going right up to the chin, including the areas that will be yellow. This gives a white base for blending the white and yellow paints together later. Include the small patch of fluffy feathers under the wings.

Now, the rest of the colors will be added on top of the white paint and blended directly on the bird. This technique produces fresh, lively colors because of tiny variations in the amount of blending in different areas.

Begin by mixing a little more white and burnt umber into the color for the underwing coverts. Dot this very pale blue-gray along the flanks and into the white under the wings with a small flat brush, such as a no. 2.

Painting Warblers • 141

Brush cadmium yellow light on the throat and upper breast. For the necklace add cadmium red medium sparingly. Cadmium red is a very powerful color, so don't overdo it. Dot a line of burnt umber above the red. Once again, use a light hand.

Clean your brush and stipple the colors together, starting at the tail and working up to the chin. This mixes the colors right on the bird. Clean your brush frequently, especially when you are working with the yellow, so you don't transfer color from one area to another. You particularly want to avoid dragging too much of a strong color into a lighter color. Dry your brush carefully after you clean it so that it is not wet with solvent, or it will lift the paint right off the bird.

Then, use the no. 1 china bristle blender to blend the colors and create the feather texture. Start from the tail and use short, light strokes in the direction the individual feathers lie on a live bird. Texture the entire underside of the bird, wiping your brush clean on a soft, lint-free cloth between every few strokes. This technique creates a subtle, feathery effect.

Next, mix a small amount of ivory black and burnt umber and use a no. 1 pointed brush to paint the lores, or dark feathers around the eye. Paint the black area slightly smaller than you want the finished patch to appear, because the black paint will be blended outward, increasing the area it covers.

Use your smallest blender, made from a no. 0 bristle brush, to carefully feather the dark paint.

Now the basic colors of the parula warbler are established. Set it aside in a safe place to dry for a day or two.

The details on the parula warbler are done with acrylic paint the same way as those on the magnolia. Begin by adding a very subtle, light edging on the flight and tail feathers.

To make the highlighting color, mix burnt umber with ultramarine blue and lighten it with titanium white to create a pale blue-gray. Dry brush this color on the edge of each feather with the no. 1 bristle blender. Begin with the top surface of the feathers, then lighten the color slightly for the feathers underneath.

Next, use the same brush to paint the wing bars on the coverts with titanium white. Make your brush strokes light and feathery. If necessary, thin the white paint with a little water for a smooth brushing consistency.

I used a no. 000 sable brush to add the white spots underneath the tail. These spots do not usually show from the top because they are only on the inner webs of the outer three tail feathers.

Make a transparent wash by mixing burnt umber and ultramarine blue, then thinning it with water to a medium blue-gray. Do not add any white to this color, or it will become opaque. Lighten it if necessary by adding more water. This wash will be used to create shadow details on the carving, and shadows are by nature transparent.

Paint this color in the wood-burned lines between the feathers of the wings and tail. This creates a shadow detail that enhances the separation between the feathers. I also use this color to paint shafts on the feathers. Because the parula's wings and tail are fanned out, more of the center shafts show than on the other two warblers. As an optional detail you can also add a few breaks in the feather barbs the same way as on the magnolia warbler.

Lighten the wash by adding more water, and paint the shadow details on the undersides of the wings and tail the same way. If you have any trouble with these acrylic washes beading up on the carving, simply add a tiny drop of dish detergent or acrylic wetting agent to break the surface tension of the water.

Painting Warblers • 145

Now, make a wash that is lighter and more blue by mixing cerulean blue with burnt umber and adding a little ultramarine blue. Test the color on a pad of white paper. It should be a shade or two darker than the blue-gray on the back of the warbler. Use this color to dry brush a little feather texture onto the blue areas of the back and wings with the no. 1 blender.

You can use the same wash to add feather texture on the undersides of the wings, but lighten it considerably by adding more water.

Always use a light touch for this step; make sure your brush leaves just light wisps of color on the carving.

If you would like to add some additional subtle feather texture to the throat, use a warmer, deeper yellow acrylic, such as Azo yellow orange, and dry brush it lightly over the throat with the no. 1 bristle blender.

Then use a tiny, pointed brush, such as a no. 000 sable, to paint the white on the eyelids. The parula warbler does not have a full eye ring, just a small crescent of white above and below the eye. Apply a thin coat of white, using only the very point of the brush.

The final step is to paint the parula warbler's beak, which differs from the magnolia's and the blackburnian's. The top mandible is dark, but the lower mandible is yellowish.

I use alkyd paint on the beak, as the slower drying time allows me to control the color very precisely. I like to apply a very thin layer of paint that lets some of the natural wood color show through.

For the top portion of the beak, use burnt umber mixed with ivory black. The bottom half is cadmium yellow medium mixed with burnt sienna. Use a small, flat no. 1 brush to apply the paint.

Then take another small, flat brush that is clean and dry (no solvents in the bristles) and use it to gently blend the paint from the base of the beak toward the tip. This step removes any excess paint, creating the translucent appearance of a warbler's beak.

If you like, you can use the no. 000 brush to paint a very fine dark line between the upper and lower mandibles when the beak is dry.

Here are some additional warbler carvings you can make using the patterns and techniques in this book.

Cerulean Warbler

Chestnut-Sided Warbler

Yellow Warbler

Black-Throated Blue Warbler

Myrtle Warbler

Common Yellowthroat

Resources

Albert Constantine & Sons, Inc.
2050 Eastchester Rd.
Bronx, NY 10461
718-792-1600
woodcarving tools and supplies

Brookstone
1655 Bassford Dr.
Mexico, MO 65265-1382
1-800-926-7000
epoxy putty

Christian J. Hummul Co.
P.O. Box 1093
Hunt Valley, MD 21030
1-800-762-0235
alkyd and acrylic paints, brushes, magnifying visors, basswood, knives, woodburning pens, glass eyes, cast feet

Detail Master Burning Systems
2650 Davisson St.
River Grove, IL 60171
708-452-5400
woodburning pens

P. C. English Enterprises
6201 Mallard Rd. Box 380
Thornburg, VA 22565
703-582-2200
basswood, glass eyes, cast feet, carving supplies

Woodcarvers Supply, Inc.
P.O. Box 7500
Englewood, FL 34295-7500
1-800-284-6229
books, woodburning pens, knives, gouges, sharpening supplies

Woodcraft
210 Wood County Industrial Park
P.O. Box 1686
Parkersburg, WV 26102-1682
1-800-225-1153
knives, gouges, sharpening supplies, woodburning pens, books, basswood

National Wood Carvers Association
7424 Miami Avenue
Cincinnati, OH 45243
dues include a subscription to Chip Chats, *a bimonthly magazine filled with projects, patterns, and regional news about woodcarving*

ABOUT THE AUTHORS

Rick Bütz, who brings some thirty years' carving experience to Stackpole's Woodcarving Step by Step series, recently served as host of the popular PBS series "Woodcarving with Rick Bütz." **Ellen Bütz** is a woodcarver, writer, and photographer; she and Rick have written numerous articles on carving for *Fine Woodworking, Woodworker's Journal, Wood Magazine,* and others. They are also the authors of *How to Carve Wood* and *Woodcarving with Rick Bütz*. They live in a log cabin in the Adirondack Mountains of New York State.